Major Truths from the Minor Prophets

Major Truths from the Minor Prophets

Power, Freedom, and Hope for Women

Edna Ellison

Kimberly Sowell

Tricia Scribner

NEW HOPE
PUBLISHERS
Gospel-Centered. Missions-Driven.

New Hope® Publishers
P. O. Box 12065
Birmingham, AL 35202-2065
newhopedigital.com

New Hope Publishers is a division of WMU®.
© 2012 by Edna Ellison, Tricia Scribner, and Kimberly Sowell
All rights reserved. First printing 2012.

Printed in the United States of America.

Library of Congress Cataloging-in-Publication Data
Scribner, Tricia.
 Major truths from the minor prophets : power, freedom, and hope for women / Tricia Scribner, Edna Ellison, and Kimberly Sowell.
   p. cm.
 ISBN 978-1-59669-324-1 (sc)
 1. Bible. O.T. Minor prophets--Textbooks. 2. Christian women--Religious life--Textbooks. I. Ellison, Edna. II. Sowell, Kimberly. III. Title.
 BS1560.S395 2012
 224'.906--dc23
                  2012019899

ISBN-10: 1-59669-324-X
ISBN-13: 978-1-59669-324-1

N0124131 • 0812 • 3M1

About the Authors

Award-winning author of 23 books and more than 400 magazine articles, *Edna Ellison* is a well-known keynote speaker and author of Bible study books. This PhD graduate from the University of Alabama has taught at Baptist seminaries and American universities. A leader in Advanced Writers and Speakers Association and a certified CLASS speaker, her life has been featured by Focus on the Family, where she has also been published.

Kimberly Sowell, founder and president of Kingdom Heart Ministries, is devoted to women's ministry. As a speaker and writer, her passion is equipping women in missions and evangelism, as her many books and studies designed for women and families attest. She serves as the director of missions mobilization and women's ministry at her home church and has a master of divinity degree from Southeastern Baptist

Theological Seminary. Kimberly has authored and edited numerous magazine articles and newsletters for evangelical groups, and has been featured on various radio and television programs.

Tricia Scribner, an evangelical Christian author and speaker, specializes in Christian apologetics as well as in mentoring and women's topics. She has authored five books and written numerous magazine articles. She holds a master of science degree in nursing from Northwestern State University and a master of arts degree in apologetics from Southern Evangelical Seminary. Tricia now works as a high school Bible teacher, teaching Old and New Testament survey, apologetics, and marriage and family courses.

Dedicated to Jesus Christ,

our Best Friend, Lord, and Savior

Table of Contents

Acknowledgments

We thank our families for helping inspire us to write and for giving of their time while we spent extended hours writing this book. Their patience was a precious gift as we researched the facts, coordinated the dates, formulated the chapters, keyed in the contents, edited the sentences, proofread each word, and prayed over the final manuscript. We are also grateful for Dr. Andrea Mullins, publisher of New Hope Publishers, for believing in us as a multigenerational team of authors; for Joyce Dinkins, managing editor, for tireless hours transforming our manuscript into a smooth, readable book; and for Michel Lê and Glynese Northam, graphic designers, who performed their God-given, magical talent to display these beautiful pages.

Introduction

beautiful friendship developed out of a community ministry board, where I first met Betty Kay. She had such a calming presence at each board meeting as the committee sat around the table to discuss what were sometimes some very difficult decisions. I was young and headstrong. I chaired the committee and therefore felt compelled to do much of the talking, even when I had little of substance to say, but not Betty Kay. She listened with great attention as ideas flew around the room. You could see her mind engaging the situation, and after much discussion by the rest of us, Betty Kay would speak. When she started to share her thoughts, I found myself drawn to her words like a moth to the light, because I knew her words were well deliberated before spoken. I knew she would say something wise and profound each time she spoke, making her rare comments well worth the wait. Though she spoke little, what she said had a profound effect on our ministry, as well as upon my heart; I eventually asked Betty Kay to be my spiritual mentor.

The Minor Prophets aren't classified as minor because their messages have been evaluated as somehow less significant. Quite the contrary, the contents of their pages speak to the soul, calling all followers of Holy God to sober living. Their messages cut to the quick of any person aware of his or her own personal sin, yet will leave the heart filled with hope. These prophets are labeled minor because of a lesser *word* count, but not a lesser *power* count. And like the one who captures your attention because of the profound contents of his hardly spoken words, allow the brief yet Spirit-directed words of the Minor Prophets to arrest your thoughts as God takes you deeper in your daily walk down a narrow path that leads to life.

Kimberly wrote the illustration of the spiritual mentor above. Tricia and Edna have also given personal illustrations throughout the book, and we have indicated the chapter authors.

In any book that required collaboration, the authors become closely joined during the writing process. We three pray this corporate prayer: that our words will point all who read this Bible study to the Savior.

CHAPTER 1

Hosea: Forgiving Husband

by Kimberly Sowell

"'I will betroth you to me forever; I will betroth you in righteousness and justice, in love and compassion. I will betroth you in faithfulness, and you will acknowledge the LORD.'" HOSEA 2:19–20

The Tater Tots and frozen chicken patties were sliding around on my baking sheet, and I was just about to slip my newlywed-style meal in the oven when the phone rang. There I stood with dinner in one hand and the phone in the other, laughing lightheartedly at the joke my loved one was playing on me. "Yeah, right. Stop kidding before your wife overhears you say that again," I said. After a minute or two of his patient persistence, I finally understood that this wasn't a bad joke. His wife was leaving him. I was speechless. It was my first experience with divorce.

A fractured relationship between a husband and wife is heartbreaking to watch and even more painful to experience, particularly when one spouse has been unfaithful. In the Book of Hosea, God used the image of an unfaithful bride to describe the unfaithfulness of the Hebrew people toward their God. The prophet Hosea carried a heavy burden in this scenario because God asked him not only to be the messenger, but to live out the message as he lived with an unfaithful wife, Gomer. The Book of Hosea is filled with heavy imagery, but in the end, this sordid narrative is a love story between the living God and the Bride of Christ.

PLAYING THE HARLOT (HOSEA 1–3)

The New Testament contains imagery of Christ as the Bridegroom and the church as His bride (John 3:29). As a Christian woman, perhaps you've embraced that role as bride of Christ and all its imagery from Scripture. You can see it in your mind's eye now: you're waiting patiently, clean and beautiful, looking out the window with joyous expectation as you wait for Jesus the Bridegroom to return. Your lamp is lit, your white bridal gown is without spot or wrinkle, and you know that Jesus will be as thrilled as you are when you finally meet face-to-face. That's how we would like to imagine ourselves as the bride of Christ; certainly not as the bride described in Hosea 1–3.

God had made a covenant with His chosen people, and they had broken covenant by committing spiritual adultery. Israel had played the harlot, sinning against God by going after other loves. Despite God's righteous anger against Israel, He expressed His love and plan of redemption even in these early chapters of Hosea. God painted a beautiful picture of the blessings that would one day come when His people returned to Him.

Jezreel was the location of a great massacre committed by King Jehu. One of Elisha's servants instructed Jehu to strike down Ahab and his whole household, but Jehu murdered far more than Ahab's bloodline, including King Ahaziah and 42 of his relatives (2 Kings 9–10). Jehu sowed the land with blood, but God would one day sow it with love and bring forth a harvest (Hosea 2:21–23).

$\mathcal{M}$AJORING ON THE MINOR PROPHET

1. How is Hosea's family described in Hosea 1? What is the spiritual significance of each child's name?

2. Read Hosea 2:5. Why was the harlot attracted to these other lovers? How are Christians sometimes deceived into thinking that something or someone besides God is fulfilling their needs?

3 Hosea 2:7 reminds us how the world will lure us, use and abuse us, and then abandon us, leaving us to deal with the pain on our own. Read Luke 15:11–32, and compare Hosea 2:7 with the prodigal son's realization while feeding the swine.

4 Examine Hosea 2:13. What is the image in this verse? How is it possible for the bride of Christ to be forgetful of her Bridegroom, Jesus?

5. In Hosea 2:14, God lures His people, drawing them away from evil pursuers and returning them to His side. How has God pursued you?

6. Compare Joshua 7:19–26 to Hosea 2:15. How did the occurrence of Joshua's day in the Valley of Achor restore hope to the Israelites?

7. When God "betrothes" us to Himself, what does God offer us (2:19–20)? How long is salvation going to last?

8. Examine Hosea 3 and think about the imagery of the husband reclaiming his bride. How do you see God described here as:

Rescuer?

Redeemer?

Restorer?

U SE YOUR IMAGINATION

1. Try to imagine a wife of Hosea's time living the adulterous lifestyle that God described in Hosea 1–3. Would she be very different from a modern-day adulterous wife?

2. What would you say to an adulterous woman to help her see her choices from her husband's perspective?

3. What would you say to a woman committing spiritual adultery to help her see her choices from God's perspective? How does this answer compare to your answer to the previous question?

CRIME AND PUNISHMENT (HOSEA 4–10)

I have lived in the South for the majority of my life. We Southerners are known for many charming ways as well as our peculiarities, but one particular mannerism of Southern women that I especially value is our appreciation for a word fitly spoken. I have watched many a Southern woman craft each word carefully as she spoke, skillfully navigating her way through a most precarious conversation filled with landmines of gossip, unwholesome words, and potential hurt feelings, and somehow step off on the other side smelling like a Georgia peach. I have studied this craft and tried to make it my own. Proverbs 25:11 (NKJV) teaches, "A word fitly spoken is like apples of gold in settings of silver."

Every word of Scripture has been weighed carefully and fitly spoken by God. No word is too harsh, no assessment askew, no observation misguided, because the Bible contains the very words of God. The words in Hosea are vivid, specific, graphic, and on target as God plainly spoke the truth about what had become of Israel. What shameful garments of truth for the betrothed of God to wear!

One simple yet profound observation God made was this: "'Israel has rejected what is good'" (8:3). Think about all that is good in God's eyes. His creation is good, all that He showers down upon us is good, and — most importantly — God is good. Have you rejected anything that God has called good?

$\mathcal{M}$AJORING ON THE MINOR PROPHET

1. Prosperity had become a stumbling block for Israel (4:7). Read Proverbs 30:8–9. How does wealth deceive? How does your heart respond to the concept of desiring only daily bread in order to avoid the temptations that come with wealth?

2. God said, "'My people are destroyed from lack of knowledge'" (4:6). This deep knowing of God, knowing Him intimately through time spent studying His ways and hearing His voice, was no longer a pursuit of the Israelites. They thought they knew God (8:2), but God was aware that their hearts were pursuing knowledge of other things. What is your greatest pursuit at this moment in your life?

3. So many Jews who lived during the days when Jesus walked the earth had the same problem; they did not know the Lord. John 1:10 says, "He was in the world, and though the world was made through him, the world did not recognize him." Today we are called to present Christ to a world who does not know Him. Can the world recognize Christ in you?

4. Hosea 6:3 (NKJV) encourages, "Let us know, let us pursue the knowledge of the Lord." Is there a difference between pursuing the Lord and pursuing knowledge of the Lord? Is there a difference between pursuing the knowledge of the Lord and the knowledge of His Word?

5. Judah is mentioned for its instability. The people of Judah had short-lived spurts of faithfulness (6:4). Think about your own walk with Christ. Are you consistent? If not, what types of circumstances tend to lure you away from faithfulness to God?

6. God called Ephraim "a cake unturned" (7:8 NKJV). What are the symptoms of being spiritually "half-baked"?

7. Hosea 4–10 contains graphic depictions of sin and the wrath of God that would be packed into Israel's punishment. In the space below, jot down the words or phrases that you find most striking. Pray and spend time pursuing the Lord's message to you through these words fitly spoken by God.

$\mathcal{U}$ SE YOUR IMAGINATION

Read the beginning of this fairytale, and then finish the story.

Once there was a charming prince who lived in a castle nestled in the beautiful hillsides of a land called Promise. His name was Faithful and True. He was the most powerful in all the land because His Father had granted it to Him.

One day the prince descended from his throne on high and entered into the village below to select a bride. There he found the bride he so greatly desired. His heart quickened for her with a love so pure. She was not of noble birth. The prince had nothing to gain from the maiden, but he desired that she would accept him because he knew how greatly he could bless her life. The maiden could never match the comeliness of the prince, but she was beautiful in his sight. He found his would-be bride in a terrible plight, enslaved to a master most cruel and himself very powerful. Yet the slave master was no match for Prince Faithful, and he bought his bride at an unspeakably high price.

When Prince Faithful and his bride began their life together, the relationship began most sweetly as they sat and talked to one another, daily drawing closer in their love. But one day, the prince noticed that his bride had begun to withdraw. She gave him very little of her attention; she had other things to attend to each day. As time progressed, the problem worsened and her affections waned. Some days the prince could see from the look in his bride's eyes that she seemed almost ashamed or afraid to be near him, which broke his heart all the more. Would his bride renew her intimacy with the prince? Would he feel her nearness once again?

How should this story end?

HAPPILY EVER AFTER (HOSEA 11-14)

Everybody loves a happy ending. When we sit down to watch a "chick flick" movie, we usually know within the first 30 minutes how the movie is going to end, but we'll gladly sit through the other 2 hours just to see the happy couple fall in love. The few times that a novel or movie has shocked me with a closing t-wist, keeping the star-crossed lovers separated forever, I found myself downright frustrated! Fictitious characters or no, everybody knows that any love story worth telling has to have a happy ending! (You can tell that *Romeo and Juliet* is not my favorite read.)

Hosea's name carries the idea of "salvation" and is written the same in Hebrew as Joshua's original name, listed in Numbers 13:16.

God must also love a happy ending, because the story of His love for His bride — as sordid and shocking as the bride's behavior may be — ends with God's redeeming love. As God shared His closing words to Israel and Judah in the Book of Hosea, we find strong glimmers of hope and encouraging words of love tucked between final proclamations of judgment. Just as God gave hope to Adam and Eve while in the process of punishing them on their way out of the garden, God offered restoration to His wayward bride in the midst of the heat of punishment. God laid bare His deep passion for His chosen people: "'How can I give you up, Ephraim? How can I hand you over, Israel? How can I treat you like Admah? How can I make you like Zeboyim? My heart is changed within me; all my compassion is aroused'" (11:8). Admah and Zeboyim were locations associated with the destruction of Sodom and Gomorrah. These were His beloved people God was talking to; He would not utterly destroy them as He did with Sodom and Gomorrah.

And why? Was God's great love earned by His people? No, they were guilty before God. They had proven themselves to be multiple offenders of spiritual adultery. We also have not earned God's love. God's patience and mercy are not so much about who we are, but more about who He is. Just as God said through the prophet Malachi: "'For I *am* the LORD, I do not change; therefore you are not consumed, O sons of Jacob'" (3:6 NKJV). God is love.

*M*AJORING ON THE MINOR PROPHET

1. God rescued Jacob's descendants, the Israelite people, from Egyptian bondage in the days of Moses. How was God giving a foreshadowing of redemption in Hosea 11:1? Which other significant figure was called out of Egypt (Matthew 2:15)?

2. God made many accusations against His people for their evil alliances. God is jealous for us to rely upon Him supremely to rescue us from our enemies. How has God been Rescuer in your life?

3. What common phrase is found in Hosea 12:9 and 13:4? When did God become Lord in your life? Why would God mark this occasion as the time He became the Lord their God?

4. God said, "'There is no Savior except Me'" (13:4). Many people have yet to find Jesus to be the one and only Savior who will redeem their souls. What is the testimony you could share with someone about how you have found Jesus to be the only true Savior?

5. Read 1 Samuel 8:4–20, the account of Israel's demand for an earthly king. Compare this passage to Hosea 13:10–11. Why did the people originally desire a king in Samuel's day? When you think about Jesus as King over your life, and as the King of kings who will reign forever, how has King Jesus shown His love and faithfulness to you?

6. Paul refers to Hosea 13:14 in 1 Corinthians 15:54–57. Read these verses. Below, write down five ways in which God has given you victory through Jesus Christ.

7. Hosea 14 offers a beautiful description of what happens when we accept God's offer of restoration, and we repent and return to Him. God instructs us to come to Him with words when we're ready to repent (v. 2). What words of repentance do you need to offer to God today?

8. Hosea 14:9 is the perfect ending to this sordid love story between a faithful Bridegroom and an unfaithful yet much cherished bride. God invites us to take the entire Book of Hosea and contextualize it to our own lives. What is the most important truth you needed to hear from the Book of Hosea

$\mathcal{U}$ SE YOUR IMAGINATION

A love note — what fun! Have you ever received one? Have you ever written one? Write a "love note" to God. Pour out your love in words to your Bridegroom, Jesus Christ.

FINAL REFLECTIONS

What a faithful Bridegroom we have in Jesus! Imagining our sins and flights of fancy as spiritual adultery helps us understand how serious our transgressions are against God, and how personally God takes our unfaithfulness. What could be so alluring as to entice us to be unfaithful to the One who has loved us with an everlasting love? God said of Israel, "'They turn to other gods and love the sacred raisin cakes'" (Hosea 3:1). Raisin cakes. Little momentary slices of pleasure. Confections for the mind, bite-sized gratification for the flesh. What are the raisin cakes in your life? Lay them at the foot of the cross.

> *Prayer: Precious Lord, You are worthy of my full attention, my faithfulness, and my love. You are worthy to be first in my life. You are my Lord, my Savior, my Redeemer, and my Friend. There is no one like You. I want to pledge myself to You as Your bride. I long to know You, my God. I want to bring honor to Your name. Your love for me is amazing. I praise You! Amen.*

JOURNAL FOR THE MAJORS IN MY LIFE:

CHAPTER 2

Joel: Faithful Dreamer

by Edna Ellison

Be not afraid . . . be glad and rejoice. Surely the Lord has done great things. JOEL 2:21

few years ago I had a terrible dream. A monster from outer space was chasing me and, though I was running as fast as possible, the monster was gaining ground. I jumped on a bus to get away from him, and it had no floor! I had to swing from a bus strap while the road flew by underneath me and all the other passengers, who didn't seem scared at all. I awakened with palms sweating and heart racing.

Some of us are afraid of bad dreams, flying in a plane, monsters, physical harm, financial disaster, or other things, but all of us are afraid of something. The story of Joel is about a terrible dream and bright hope in the midst of fear.

JOEL: FEARFUL DREAMER? (JOEL 1:1–12)

We usually dream about things we fear. Have you ever dreamed about something chasing you, destroying everything around you, or awakened with your muscles straining from running in a dream? If so, you are not alone.

Like all of us, Joel had fears.

Joel lived in a land where hoards of locusts invaded periodically and devoured most of the crops, leaving famine and devastation. We can assume Joel had seen plagues of locusts before. He knew how dark the sky could become as they swarmed overhead and blocked out the sun; he had heard the roaring sound as they came nearer and nearer, and he could still smell the stench of all the dead plants and small animals after they had ravaged the landscape, smothering and devouring everything in their path. We can imagine how he shuddered the night he dreamed of another horde of the insects filling the skies.

Read Joel 1:1–12. The first verse doesn't paint a perfect picture of Joel's dream or vision. It simply calls his revelation "the word of the Lord." What an understatement, since his imagery of this terror is so vivid!

In these verses, Joel presents the fearsome picture of Judah's future destruction, which has survived other wars. He calls specific people in Judah to pray and mourn over sins in the region. Joel is not the son of a king or prophet. He simply is a man called by God to speak for Him.

Imagine how you would feel if God called you to share a prophecy. Would you say, "Thanks, God, and where's the

BACKGROUND

Joel, which means "Yahweh, or the LORD, is God," was a common name in Old Testament Judah. It combines the covenant name of God, *Jehovah*, with the main word for God, *el*, thus: *Jo-el*. We know few facts about the prophet Joel except that his father was Pethuel, and that he lived in Judah and may have been associated with the Jerusalem temple. Some Bible scholars think the Book of Joel was written around 830 B.C., in the days when King Joash ruled and Jehoiada, the high priest, was regent in Judah. You can find a painting of the prophet Joel on the ceiling of the Sistine Chapel. There Michelangelo painted him with white hair, partially bald, seated in a temple, reading a scroll.

nearest exit?" Which kinds of prophecies would you welcome? Some Christians know they have the natural talents, learned skills, or spiritual gifts that would make prophesying easy. What would be your ideal task if God calls you, like Joel, to speak for Him?

Most of us might hesitate, feeling unequal to the task, without courage to take a stand for righteousness. Which life situations do you see that need addressing in today's world? Would they fall under family sins, political failures, religious clashes, or cultural issues? Consider today how many problems would diminish — or even disappear — if every Christian took up the challenge to make a difference. Regardless of the task, God never calls us to do things without equipping us or giving us the courage to accomplish His purposes.

*M*AJORING ON THE MINOR PROPHET

Imagine Joel's heart when he recognized the "word of the Lord" that came to him (Joel 1:1). Could he have awakened in fear, with sweaty palms and fluttering heart palpitations? We don't know how long he hesitated before sharing his vision. Confronting his feelings, he began telling everyone about this word he had received from God.

1. How long do you think Joel delayed before he spoke to others about his vision?

Whom does Joel warn about the oncoming crisis?

2. How do you think the young widows' reaction in verse 8 differs from the "drunkards" mentioned in verse 5?

   How might other groups react?

3. "Elders" (v. 2) and "priests" (v. 9) are leadership titles still used today. Name titles for other clergy or laity who might represent this category of worshipers today.

   Notice that Joel uses the imperative verbs, "Hear this," and "listen." Given the urgency of his commands, do you think today's leadership bears special responsibility?

4. What do people in questions 1 through 3 have in common?

5. How would you feel if one of your friends, like Joel, explained such a vision to you?

U SE YOUR IMAGINATION

Imagine you are Joel — or a woman in Joel's day. Use your imagination in the following two questions. Since there are no wrong or right answers, enjoy the activities below.

1. Michelangelo pictures Joel as an older man. How do you picture him?

If you have artistic talent, draw/paint a picture of Joel, as you see him. (See sidebar.) Then go online http://en.wikipedia.org/wiki/Joel/(prophet), or to a library and find a picture of the Sistine Chapel ceiling fresco, 1508–1512. Compare your image to that of Michelangelo.

2. Joel uses figurative language in his description of the locusts (in the grass-hopper family) with teeth, running like a foreign nation's foot soldiers as they destroy Judah. Using phrases from other verses describing the locusts' damage to the land, write a poem — rhymed or unrhymed — about the scene Joel faced. Begin with a basic sentence containing a simile (a comparison using *like* or *as*), such as "My work is like a big monster that bites," or "My house is like a garden. The dust grows larger daily." In your poem of hope, compare your situation to Joel's, ending with the theme of God's love and forgiveness.

Example:

JOEL'S HOPE
Some days at my house locusts take the land
And like wild things my chores are close at hand.
My children, spouse, or neighbors bring despair,
Or smell of burned-up roast hangs in the air.
But I remember Joel saw the truth
And afterward, the old men and the youth
Saw visions and dreamed dreams that would abound.
And God restored their fortunes and their ground
And poured His Spirit out on young and old,
Enabling them to feel hope — strong and bold.

Just like the Hebrew children I can fear
On dreary days that offer me no cheer,
And selfish and depressed because of sin,
Sometimes I feel pent up and then penned in.
The Valley of Decision's here today

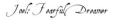
As I remember Joel's message say,

"God loves His people; He'll a refuge be,

And everyone who calls his name is free!"

When I am weak, I then say "I am strong!"

Like Joel I proclaim Him all day long!

JOY THAT WITHERS AWAY (JOEL 1:13 TO 2:17)

All of us experience dry times. (We're delusional if we protest that we remain joyful every moment!) How can we approach dry days — or disastrous times when all seems lost?

Read Joel 1:13, 16–20. Like us, Joel experienced a dry period in his life. The condition of the land is symbolic of his inner spirit. How does his mood change from verse 12 to 13? As he urges the priests to show leadership before the rest of the people,

> **FUN FACT**
>
> According to the *Dream Moods A to Z Dream Dictionary*, everyone dreams, though we may not remember our dreams, as Joel did. If you see locusts in your dream, it may represent transformation, or you may be indecisive about something. <www.dreammoods.com/dreaminformation/dreamfacts.htm>

he gives us several suggestions on how to face a dry period before, during, or after a crisis in our lives. Read verse 13 again, and record in your journal the suggestions there and in verses 14–15. Fasting and praying can help us focus on God. Placing physical concerns aside for a designated period, we can consider more closely our place in God's plan. Our reflections become more personal as we meditate on Christ rather than on possessions, home, family responsibilities, work, or even church business. Look for other suggestions in Joel 2:1–17. Write all of these in your journal.

Joel 2:12–14 are three of the most hopeful verses in the Old Testament. Even though Joel faithfully relays the fearsome details of his vision from God, he's also trustworthy in portraying the true nature of God, a forgiving, loving deity.

*M*AJORING ON THE MINOR PROPHET

1. What does Joel suggest people do?

2. Which verse in Joel 2:12–14 touches your heart most?

    Which verse seems like an unrealistic wish?

3. What does Joel say to your heart about an *inner* crisis rather than an *outer* one?

4. Verses 15–16 are directed to leaders. How do these words translate to modern leaders?

Write here what you think these words mean in today's in today's world filled with electronic technology:

$\mathcal{U}$SE YOUR IMAGINATION

Imagine God is placing you in the 800s B.C., giving you a dream like Joel's. As you observe all sorts of people in that era, thank God for varied biblical examples, so that people in the twenty-first century can see mistakes as well as good behavior in Bible characters. Pray He'll soften your heart for people in Israel today as well as in Joel's day.

Ask God for one special blessing from this study as His gift to bless your life and lead you closer to His heart.

1. As one of the women described in Joel 1 and 2. How could you react to this urgent crisis in the land?

    Given the status of women in the Old Testament, what choices could you make?

2. As an advocate for children, what actions would you take in Joel's situation?

3. Using Joel 2:14, how would you advise a friend today who needs hope in God's mercy?

4. As a leader, how can you carry Joel's wisdom to people of all ages and lifestyles in your church?

5. If you are not an active leader, how could you use these words to advise your church?

SALVATION IN THE LORD (JOEL 2:18 TO 3:21)

Joel 2 and 3 contain one of the most miraculous passages of the Bible, presenting a glimpse of Christ's salvation hundreds of years before He was born! Read Joel 2:18–27. The Lord shows His desire for relationship with His people, promising never to make them an object of scorn among other nations, encouraging them not to be *afraid*, but *glad* because of the great things God has done. Then He gives them the ultimate promise, which all of us who have suffered need to hear: "I will repay you for the years the locusts have eaten" (2:25).

Next God tells of a period of physical and spiritual plenty. The Judean people will have plenty to eat, but much more importantly, they'll have abundant *spirit* to sustain them. He promises to pour out the Holy Spirit on not just a few prophets or priests but on all people. Many men and women

"will prophesy. . . dream dreams. . . see visions" (v. 28). Then God foretells the coming of Jesus Christ as Savior: "And everyone who calls on the name of the Lord will be saved . . . there will be deliverance" (2:32).

Chapter 3 begins with God's gathering all nations to the Valley of Jehoshaphat (v. 2), or the Valley of Decision (v. 14) where He judges them. The chapter promises justice for those who had engaged in dishonesty, gambling, and human trafficking, and then offers hope: God will empower the weak to stand against God's enemies for justice. He ends the passage (v. 21) with a promise to be near, as a refuge and stronghold for His people, with guilt and sin pardoned at last.

*M*AJORING ON THE MINOR PROPHET

1. Through which two human characteristics in Joel 2:18 does God show He wants to have a personal relationship with you?

   Does God have the right to be jealous of you or the way you use your time, energy, and possessions? How will you respond to His jealousy and pity?

2. Verses 19 and 26 refer to humiliation. Have you ever been humiliated?

How has God replaced your feelings of shame with feelings of power and enthusiasm for righteousness?

How will you share this with others as a testimony about God?

3. How may God repay a person for "the years the locusts have eaten" (v. 25)?

4. Write in your journal your favorite promises in Joel.

5. Which words in Joel 2:28–32 show that God does not discriminate, regardless of social status, gender, nationality, or culture?

U SE YOUR IMAGINATION

It's hard for us to imagine the stress on people in Joel's day. We know many lived in fear because of invasions from stronger nations. Women also lived in fear, waiting on their fathers or husbands to take care of them, since they had no status of their own and were often abused or raped. Most couldn't own property, be the head of a household, or speak to men other than their husbands; and some were offered as concubines in business deals or political treaties. They must have been terrified to realize Joel's prophecy of war and destruction was from the Lord.

1. If you were a Jewish woman living in Joel's day, do you think you would be one of those punished or blessed through the crisis? Give reasons for your answer in your journal.

2. God says "Let the weak say, 'I am strong!'" How does a Christian grow from weakness to strength?

What advice would you give someone who says she could never be a strong witness or powerful evangelist for the Lord?

3. Which phrases in Joel 3:3 do you think refer to gambling and human trafficking?

How does lifestyle in Joel's day compare to lifestyles today?

What is your desire about influencing lives in those situations?

4. God says to prepare for war (3:9). How do you believe you can prepare for spiritual warfare in your life?

5. Reread Joel 3:14. Do you think the Lord is always near us in a Valley of Decision?

Why or why not? Do you believe you may be in a Valley of Decision now?

What decision involving change in your life is God nudging you to make?

6. Spend time today thanking God for pardoning you for sin. Ask forgiveness for times you held onto guilt after you could have released it. Celebrate with Joel's words in this study to give you hope.

FOR FURTHER STUDY

Most of us can relate to the Prophet Joel, imagining how he must have felt when God called him as a messenger to His people. Have you ever felt God call you to present His message? Did He nudge you to tell others at school, home, or church about His love? Did he call you to tell your family? Were you afraid? How are you like Joel? Remember, most great leaders felt hesitant or awkward when they first took responsibility. Read the stories of Samuel (1 Samuel 3:2–21), and David (1 Samuel 16:1–13; 17:38–39), and compare your servant leadership or obedience to share. May you overcome every fear, make godly decisions, and celebrate the hope that Joel offers.

> *Prayer: Almighty God, help us not to fear anything, whatever the circumstance of our lives. Thank You for giving us a total trust in You, a deep peace during every life-storm, and a solid hope in the future. Give us courage to face any crisis with serenity, and equip us to serve You one day at a time. In Jesus' name, Amen.*

*J*OURNAL FOR THE MAJORS IN MY LIFE:

CHAPTER 3

Amos: Plumb Line Among People

by Edna Ellison

Then the Lord said, "Look, I am setting a plumb line among my people Israel." Amos 7:8

My father, Deany Martin, worked as a carpenter for my great-uncle Ellie Poole, a contractor. Each morning Daddy carried his handmade toolbox to work, returning it nightly to a cherished shelf. If he worked on more than one home site, he carried the box with him. I loved looking at the thingamajigs in his box. Occasionally he demonstrated them to my brother and me, teaching us to respect them.

Once I went with Daddy to the business workshop. As he waited to use a certain kind of saw, he asked me to help measure two boards. He slid one board into a grove on the other and stood them on end. "We need to make sure they're plumb."

"Plumb? Are you a plumber?"

He grinned. "No, I'm a carpenter." He picked a pointed steel plumb-bob from his toolbox, holding it by a cord above the boards. "Gravity makes this plumb-bob hang straight," he explained, "so the board will be at right angles to the floor."

He rubbed a piece of blue chalk down the plumb line. I held the plumb-bob to the bottom of one board. He held the line taut at the top. Then he popped the line against the board—making a straight chalk line all the way down—and sawed one inch off the board, equal at every point along the blue line.

Like carpenters' boards, our lives are warped or level, straight or crooked, unmarred or flawed. As Christians, we measure ourselves against a perfect standard, Jesus Christ. We often search His Word for true measures for life.

AMOS: SHEPHERD FROM JUDAH (AMOS 1–3)

God uses ordinary people in everyday jobs as timeless symbols of His principles for living. Amos was one of those, a simple shepherd. Read Amos 1:1, a small verse containing a history book of information. From a small town, Tekoa, Amos received God's message two years before a giant earthquake hit. (8.2 on the Richter scale. See Background information). Isaiah, Micah, and Hosea were Amos's contemporaries.

Although God gave Amos this message to warn about three or four sins, He listed many more. God had already given the count of three, and the people had struck out. Read Amos 1:2–13, noting passages that refer to human trafficking. Israel, guilty of buying and selling other humans, had also disregarded the civilized way of communicating with its neighbors through national treaties and covenants. They had sunk to an *all-time low*.

Verses 11–13 must have pierced many Israelites' hearts. The passage refers to relatives, perhaps brother against brother, not just in angry words, or even a fist fight, but a war with swords! The Hebrew word translated "brother" indicates the enemy was someone with the looks and characteristics of the Israeli warrior. These verses take us from the bloody battle outside to the uncompassionate fury inside people's hearts—even to the point of destroying unborn children!

Read chapter 2. Notice how many sins God holds against Moab. The Moabites were anarchists who worshiped false gods of their ancestors. The Hebrew word for "false gods" can mean "lies." Can you remember any lies told in your family or community? As each of us considers our own leftover guilt from our family's past, we can relate to people in Amos's day. As you read, note in your journal the sexual sins as well as abuse of the poor. What kind of spiritual sins in verses 5–12 are also common today?

Read chapter 3, looking for signs that God still wanted to bless His chosen people, but His patience was wearing thin. After God warns foreign people, He sets specific punishment for Israelites in the Northern Kingdom. Do you think God feels responsible for instilling obedience in His own children, who had received His blessings for decades? How could that requirement apply to your family/community?

Near the end, God warns His people about their housing. As you read near the end of chapter 3, allow God to call attention to our similar excesses today.

MAJORING ON THE MINOR PROPHET

When you were a child, did your mother count to three when she expected you to

BACKGROUND

Amos was a nomadic herdsman from Tekoa, a small town between Jerusalem and Bethlehem, probably a security outpost on the cliff above the vast Dead Sea Valley. Though Tekoa was in the Southern Kingdom of Judah, God sent Amos to announce God's judgment on Israel, the Northern Kingdom. Scholars think the Book of Amos was written during or just after his ministry, from 760-750 B.C., when King Uzziah ruled in Judah and Jeroboam II ruled in Israel. This period of peace and prosperity—especially in Israel—was extremely depraved. God called Amos to condemn the social corruption, insisting on justice on behalf of poor, exploited people.

In a famous speech made at the Golden Calf temple in Bethel, Israel, Amos warned of God's judgments on Israel's neighbors (1:1 to 2:5), and then on Israel itself (2:6 to 5:17). He announced the Hebrew exile (5:18 to 6:14), gave God's visions of divine justice (7:1 to 9:10), and predicted future restoration of Israel (9:11-15).

obey? Most children ignore the first two numbers, scurrying to be obedient by the dreaded "three." Reread Amos 1:3, 6, 9, 11, 13; and 2:1, 4, 6. Amos's account of God's warning may remind you of the "three-strikes-and-you're-out rule we often follow today.

Two years later, archaeologists estimate an 8.2 earthquake along the Dead Sea Transform Fault Zone ripped across the land, destroying buildings from today's Lebanon (the epicenter) southward—below the Dead Sea. It probably "ruptured along more than 400 kilometers as the ground shook violently for over 90 seconds!" <www.icr.org/articles/5143 (8/15/2010)>.

1. How would you reword Amos's warning for a twenty-first-century audience?

2. What would you say to women like you in the following places?

    Damascus (v. 3):

Gaza (v. 6):

Tyre (v. 9):

Edom (v. 11):

Moab (2:1):

Judah (v. 4)

Israel (v. 6)

3. Name a few biblical symbols used in chapters 1–3, which are meaning-ful to you:

4. Using Amos 1:11–13 as a comparison, what kind of "swords" do *we* use on the streets?

5. Does your nightly news portray truth?

   How could you change your world of advertising/propaganda?

6. Find in verse 6 the repeated theme of abuse of poor people. In verses 5–12, which kind of spiritual or physical sins happen today?

7. Several verses refer to human trafficking. Statistics show there are more slaves in the world today than in 1860 (more than 27,000 in the US alone). What can Christian women do about women and children in sexual or domestic slavery today?

   How is awareness a factor toward action?

8. In chapter 3, how could God's attitude about his own children apply to your life?

FOR FURTHER STUDY

Read more about Amos's environment below, taking notes in your journal.

- 2 Samuel 14:1–33. Considering what the woman from Tekoa did to help David forgive Absalom, do you think it was a place of godliness? Why?

- 1 Kings 12:28–33. Why might Amos find Jeroboam's work with golden calves distasteful?

- Zechariah 14:5. Why is it important that Zechariah's prophecy, included in the canon that became our Bible, mentions the giant earthquake?

- 2 Kings 14:21–29. What do you learn here that you didn't learn from Amos?

$\mathcal{U}$SE YOUR IMAGINATION

1. Choose one of the following people who may seem like you:

   a) Amos's mother, a poor shepherdess who watched her son leave their hometown, Tekoa, to go "up north" to Bethel to warn people there.

   b) A woman with a winter house near the Dead Sea and a summer house on the heights near Jerusalem, uphill from Tekoa.

c) A woman brutal-
ized in the temple
by idol worship-
pers — who longs
for the peaceful
past when she
could worship
God.

Write a journal/diary
entry from one woman
above.

2. Based on others as well as Amos, write in your journal a short play
about these prophets who lived at the same time as they interacted in
the Northern and Southern Kingdoms. [Considering their personali-
ties, what would each of them say to each other?] Act out the play for
your study group or other age levels in your church.

COMPLACENCY, COMPASSION, AND CALL TO REPENT (AMOS 4–6)

Although Amos 4 presents a dismal picture of this sinful nation, it also provides advice on seeking the Lord. As you read, make notes about the situation caused by God's own people's sin. Amos portrays Israelites in almost-comical illustrations in these verses, especially when they're drinking. These scenes may remind you of a movie, or program on live streaming. Amos steps on our toes, reminding us of signs God has given that it is time for repentance. God gave the Israelites an array of opportunities for ministry.

Read Amos 5, God's sad lament and His call to repentance. As he speaks, Amos promises the Israelites, if they seek the Lord, they will live (5:4). He shows God's divine nature is good, not evil (v. 14). He predicts God will place them between a lion and a bear (v. 19). Today you might say, "between a rock and a hard place" — not a good position to be in, with God as justice-giver! One of the most beautiful passages of this Bible book is verse 24, "But let justice roll on like a river, righteousness like a never-failing stream," a favorite of Dr. Martin Luther King Jr.

Though God promises hope, the bottom line is clear: He is sure to send them into exile, far "beyond Damascus," an outlying, northernmost city.

Read Amos 6, a warning against complacency. God aptly describes the wealthy: "notable men of the foremost nation" (v. 1), lying on "beds inlaid with ivory" and couches, dining on "lambs and fattened calves" (v. 4), who "strum away on harps and [other] musical instruments" (v. 5), drinking "wine by the bowlful," and using the "finest lotions" (v. 6). Look over this chapter, searching for other evidence of pride among God's people. How God's heart must have been breaking over His people, who had ignored Him and others, seeking only their own selfish comfort.

*M*AJORING ON THE MINOR PROPHET

1. Amos doesn't mince words as he lays out God's judgment against Israel. How would you translate the words of Amos 4:1 and 6:4–6*a* into the

brand-names of products used by the "good old boys" or today's fashionable women?

2. Which similar ministry opportunities do Christians have today?

3. Why do you think God says in Amos 6:7 "Therefore you will be among the first to go into exile"?

4. Which punishment in chapter 6 is most offensive to you? Why?

How can we avoid such an outcome?

*U*SE YOUR IMAGINATION

Pray, asking God to give you a vision for your community.

1. Imagine you are a woman who has become a gourmet cook and wine connoisseur. Is God fair? Why or why not?

2. How do you believe a young Israeli mother would have felt in such a situation?

   How can women today use influence in our community's institutions to make a better place in which to rear children?

3. How would you advise a friend today who has read the Book of Amos and needs hope in God's mercy?

AMOS, AMAZIAH, AND
THE CONSPIRACY THEORY (AMOS 7–9)

Ending Amos's prophecy, chapters 7–9 give us several object lessons for teaching spiritual truths. Amos first suggested several terrible actions God might take. Read chapter 7. One by one, God considered certain actions, but decided not to use them. Considering swarms of locusts and consuming fires, He realized he'd waited long enough. His righteous presence couldn't look on such evil. It was time to level the playing field with a plumb line (v. 7). He gave Amos a vision of a wall, built true to plumb. The 90-degree angles were perfect because the mason had set the wall straight as he set up his plumb line to build it.

Imagine God saying, "Amos, right is right, and wrong is wrong. I'm going to set the country straight." Amos knew what he had to do.

Look closely at 7:10–17. Amos must have been shaking in his sandals when he delivered these stark words to Bethel's high priest, Amaziah, but he was calm, standing stalwart to proclaim the message God called him to deliver. [It didn't help Amos's fast-beating heart that Amaziah had told King Jeroboam that Amos was raising a conspiracy against the throne!] Even after Amaziah shouted, "Get out, you seer!" (v. 12), Amos explained that he didn't ask for this job, but when God called him, he had to do it.

Read chapters 8 and 9, searching for the following object lessons: a basket of ripe fruit, cheating with dishonest scales, sackcloth and ashes, shaking pillars near the altar/in a house (of Israel), grains of sand in a sieve, and plowing and planting vineyards.

Write in today's journal what you think each symbol meant.

THE END OF THE STORY

Amos's prophecy came true. God used the plumb line to measure His people's faith and righteousness. He separated the self-seeking ones from the God fearing with a line of demarcation, allowing a few whom He spared to go into exile and, years later, to return to reestablish His kingdom in the Promised Land.

MAJORING ON THE MINOR PROPHET

1. In figurative language like God's to Amos, is your wall *plumb* — that is, *straight, upright*?

2. Explain how any Christian's life can be out of kilter without his or her knowing it:

3. How can people today return to the Master Mason for rebuilding our walls?

4. In Amos 8:12, sinners search for God's word. What happens?

    Why do you think they are staggering? (Are they under the influence of anything? Anyone?)

5. Why do you believe they couldn't find the Lord's word?

6. In Amos 9:1–10, is God saying that *none* — even in the temple, faithful believers — will escape by their own power? Why not?

7. How do verses 11–15 contrast with earlier verses?

$\mathcal{U}$ SE YOUR IMAGINATION

1. What are your hopes for rebuilding/restoration today? In your journal, write a paragraph or a poem about hope (Or draw an abstract picture that represents hope). Share with study-group partners.

2. The plumb line, a common tool in Old and New Testament carpenters' boxes, is a remarkable symbol of setting the standard. What's in *your* toolbox for twenty-first century living that might be similar to the plumb line in the 700s B.C.?

3. Amos told the priest at Bethel (7:14) he was bivocational: a shepherd who also tended the sycamore-fig trees (7:14). Sheep grazed on the dry high plains near Tekoa, but figs grew only in the valley near the Dead Sea. Amos probably spent many nomadic nights praying about God's message. Search your soul quietly, writing in your journal Amos's message for you.

4. What decision involving life changes is God nudging you to make?

FUN FACTS

In Amos's day the Olympic Games, which began in 776 B.C., were being held in Olympia, Greece. After 16 years of growing popularity, the people in Bethel might have heard of the faraway Olympics when Amos's ministry began in 760 B.C. Imagine Olympic Game participants' views of Amos's outrageous prophecy. Some may have felt fear. Some probably scoffed, feeling they could survive anything.

5. Read the Fun Facts sidebar. If you were Greek, how would you feel about Amos?

Prayer: Almighty God, help us see ourselves in Amos. Give us courage to stand for honesty and godliness. Forgive us for materialism and self-trust. Thank You for blessing us with peace and prosperity. May we use Your resources to bless others. Amen.

JOURNAL FOR THE MAJORS IN MY LIFE:

CHAPTER 4

Obadiah: Messenger to Feuding Brothers

by Kimberly Sowell

"As you have done, it will be done to you; your deeds will return upon your own head." OBADIAH 15

The Hatfield and McCoy feud of the late 1800s was bloody and infamous. The tales of rage, cruelty, stubbornness, and revenge — some true and some legend — have left a mark on American culture that nary a Hatfield or McCoy would relish. No matter which family triumphed from skirmish to skirmish, neither family earned the respect of American culture. Ironically, the fathers of the clans, Captain William Anderson Hatfield and Randolph McCoy, both survived the feud, while many of their family members died tragically.

Early in the timeline of mankind, twin boys named Jacob and Esau entered the world. Esau came first, with Jacob not far behind, grabbing the heel of Esau as he exited the womb (Genesis 25:26). The feud had begun. Ironically, Jacob and Esau managed not to kill each other, making peace in the end, but their descendants would not know this same peace. Tragedy would come.

The Edomites were descendants of Esau, son of Isaac and twin of Jacob. God made a covenant with Abraham, which was passed down to his son Isaac, and then passed down to Isaac's son Jacob, bypassing Esau. Sibling rivalry was the norm between the twins, and Esau even schemed in his heart to take Jacob's life (Genesis 27:41). Jacob and Esau eventually made peace with each other (Genesis 33), but the contention between their descendants would not cease.

God knew that Jacob's and Esau's descendants would continually strive with each other, a problem that began in their mother's womb. When their mother Rachel struggled in carrying the twins, God explained to her why there was such unusual activity in her womb. "The LORD said to her, 'Two nations are in your womb, and

IN FOR A BIG SURPRISE (OBADIAH 1–9)

The Edomites seemed to be holding it all together. They were a people who appeared to have the world at their fingertips. All of Edom's accomplishments had led them to arrogance, which would make their demise all the more painful. In verse 3, God warned, "'The pride of your heart has deceived you.'" Edom was in for a big surprise.

God knew what Edom possessed, and they would lose in all counts. They had the security of a home in the hill country, but God would bring them low. They had great wealth, but they would be plundered until the last grape was plucked from the vine. They had allies, but their friends would be God's tools of vengeance. They had men revered as wise and strong, but their mighty men would be slaughtered.

MAJORING ON THE MINOR PROPHET

Obadiah received a vision from God of the great destruction of an entire people. As you consider these first words of the prophecy, try to imagine receiving this vision through the eyes of Obadiah. The Edomites were relatives of the children of Israel, yet they had aligned themselves with the enemies of God's people.

two peoples from within you will be separated; one people will be stronger than the other, and the older will serve the younger'" (Genesis 25:23). Esau was the father of the nation of Edom, while Jacob's descendants would be known as the nation of Israel. (God changed Jacob's name to Israel in Genesis 32:28, thus the Hebrews are often called the children of Israel.)

1. Sometimes those who oppress God's people seem to be untouchables—beyond the reach of the long arm of the law. Have you made peace with God's sovereignty in exacting justice? Why is faith required to accept God's promise in Hebrews 10:30?

2. Verse 7 contains a chilling message of conspiracy. Edom's allies would turn against them. The betrayers would be betrayed. Have you ever experienced the betrayal of a betrayer? Have you ever befriended someone who talked down about a former friend, only to find yourself her next victim?

3. Verse 8 prophesies about the destruction of the wise men of Edom. The wisdom of this world is utter nonsense beside the deep wisdom of God. Read the following verses that pertain to wisdom. Then consider, what is the knowledge or wisdom that you spent the most effort pursuing? When you need information or guidance, what are the sources of wisdom you consult?

Proverbs 26:12

Jeremiah 8:9

1 Corinthians 1:19

1 Corinthians 3:19

$\mathcal{U}$SE YOUR IMAGINATION

Imagine a city nestled in the cliffs of rugged mountains, high above the earth below, and its people looking down on the world like an eagle perched upon her nest. You are one of these proud Edomites, and you have treasures in your sanctuaries and greatly respected leaders in and out of your gates. Your belly is full, you hear your children playing in the background, and all is well tonight. You see in the distance your allies approaching your foothills. Then another army of allies begins to appear from another direction. You feel taken off guard. You turn to see your visiting allies, the warriors and men you have been breaking bread with at your own table this night, and they now stand behind you with sword drawn. What is happening? Is this a joke? Your allies have the look of hunger for blood in their eyes — is it your blood they are craving to spill?

Jot down the sights, sounds, and emotions of the moment. In this situation, whom would a godless people turn to for help?

BROTHER AGAINST BROTHER (OBADIAH 10–14)
What had these Edomites done to cause the wrath of God to fall upon their heads? They had mistreated God's chosen people. In His covenant with

Abraham, God said of His chosen people, "'I will bless those who bless you, and whoever curses you I will curse'" (Genesis 12:3). During those times when the children of Israel rebelled against God, He chastened them, often allowing other nations to plunder and oppress them, but the Edomites crossed a line by taking pleasure in the chastisement of the Hebrews. They should have known better than to interfere with God's people, but they took lightly God's promise to "curse those who curse." They took advantage of the Hebrews' times of weakness to further injure the already-wounded Hebrews, and God took notice.

Oppressing the children of Israel was reason enough for God to pour out His wrath upon the Edomites, but their blood kinship only made their behavior sting all the worse. How could they turn against their own relatives? How could they treat the children of Israel with such coldness and cruelty? Though the Edomites and children of Israel were two distinct people groups, and God had chosen to send the covenant promise through the children of Israel instead of the Edomites, God required the children of Israel to respect the Edomites. God's instructions were clear: "'do not despise an Edomite, for the Edomites are related to you'" (Deuteronomy 23:7).

When a mother deals with the misbehavior of her child, she is willing to inflict temporary discomfort on her child in order to help the child learn. However, no mother will tolerate a stranger interfering to inflict further hardship on her child! Similarly, Obadiah's vision was God's declaration that He was going to keep His promise to Abraham (Genesis 12:3). God was willing to allow His people times of hardship when they disobeyed, but God would not tolerate any outside interference against His people.

*M*AJORING ON THE MINOR PROPHET

1. The Edomites gawked at the ugly scene while their Hebrew brothers were taken captive, taking in every detail of the carnage. When God's people suffer the consequences of their own sin, how does God want us to respond to the media and gossip? How does Proverbs 24:17–18 apply?

2. While the Hebrews were crumbling in distress, the Edomites were spouting proud words. What prideful comments do you hear people say when they talk of people who have been caught in their sin? How does 1 Corinthians 10:12 apply?

3. The Edomites were fellow looters with those who conquered the Hebrews. Can you think of a modern-day example of people financially benefiting from those who are losing their wealth as a punishment for their sinful choices?

4. Verse 14 is a disturbing picture that is hard to imagine. With death and destruction all around, with the children of Israel running for their lives, the Edomites assisted the attacking nation by stand-

    FAST FACT
    Esau was first identified by the name Edom in Genesis 25:30 when Esau sold his birthright for a red stew. "Edom" means "red."

    ing guard to round up any Israelites who would have otherwise escaped. Read Proverbs 1:10–19; how does this passage apply to the Edomites? What is God saying to you about the company you keep?

*U*SE YOUR IMAGINATION

It is not uncommon to witness the demise of men and women who suffer devastating consequences because of their sinful choices. Imagine the following scenarios unfolding. How would you respond? Would you feel strongly enough to persuade others to respond in the same manner?

1. The scandal of a minister caught in an adulterous relationship

2. The resignation of a politician who was caught participating in illegal behavior

3. The fall of a foreign nation's leader because his people rebelled against his tyrannous rule

4. The suspension of a co-worker who has been badmouthing you to the boss

5. The failure of a ministry in the church because the church member in charge stubbornly ran the ministry in the ground

REAPING WHAT YOU'VE SOWN (OBADIAH 15-21)

Occasionally consequences sneak up on you. You wouldn't have ordered the beef tips had you an inkling you were about to get food poisoning. You would have sunbathed a bit longer and skipped the dip had you known about the jellyfish that were waiting to swim with you. There may be a few invitations for blind dates you would like to have as do-overs. But consequences for our sin? We should never be surprised when we suffer because of our poor choices. Paul laid it on the line for every reader of God's Word: "Do not be deceived, God is not mocked; for whatever a man sows, that he will also reap" (Galatians 6:7 NKJV).

Obadiah's vision indicated the Edomites would be taken off guard by their impending fall (v. 7), but the Edomites were foolish to think they could be cruel to their Israelite brothers and walk away unscathed. They were going to be served the very same dish they had served: "'As you have done, it will be done to you; your deeds will return upon your own head'" (v. 15).

MAJORING ON THE MINOR PROPHET

A significant aspect of Edom's destruction was also God's restoration of Israel. As Edom fell, God's people would once again triumph. Respond to the specific prophesies that God gave through Obadiah.

1. **"There shall be deliverance"** (v. 17 NKJV). What is your testimony of God's deliverance in your life? How has God rescued you from evildoers? How has God rescued you from your own sin?

2. **"There shall be holiness"** (v. 17 NKJV). Think about God declaring that holiness shall be present in your life. Do you long for holiness? What would be the great rewards of holiness? What would you have to abandon in order to truly experience God's holiness?

3. **That which was taken from the children of Israel shall be restored (v. 17).** What has been taken from you? How would your life change if God chose to bring restoration? Are you willing to allow God to bring restoration into your life, however He deems best?

4. **The children of Israel will thrive like a flame (v. 18).** Have you asked God to give you a faith and a passion for Him that is like an unquenchable fire? Have you ever possessed such a zeal for God?

5. **The Edomites will be nothing more than stubble (v. 18).** In Matthew 3:1–12, John the Baptist used similar imagery as he spoke to the hypocritical Pharisees and Sadducees. They loved being religious but had no desire to humble themselves in service and obedience to the Lord. Read Matthew 3:1–12. What is ahead for those who do not serve Jesus as Lord?

6. **God will accomplish His plan with precision (vv. 19–20).** Only God can be so bold as to give a detailed prophesy about the fall of Edom and the restoration of the Israelites, because only God can guarantee His plans. God reigns. No one can stand against His authority. Do you fully trust God to lead you step-by-step toward victory in your life?

7. **The LORD will appoint deliverers to govern, and God Himself shall reign (v. 21).** Read Matthew 19:28–29: Luke 19:11–27: and 2 Timothy 2:12. What is the promise of God? Are you living like one who will be given this privilege by God's hand of mercy and grace?

$\mathcal{U}$ SE YOUR IMAGINATION

If you were one of the Hebrews who had suffered because of the Edomites, and you were hearing this vision of all that was to come, what would be the sweetest sentence of this prophecy? Would you be more excited about the destruction coming to the Edomites, or the restoration coming to you and your people? Write your thoughts below.

$\mathcal{F}$ INAL REFLECTIONS

As Obadiah 15 prophesies, the day of the LORD for all nations is certainly near. God will pour out His judgment and the enemies of God will feel the full wrath of God's fury. And yet . . . "the Lord is not slow in keeping his promise, as some understand slowness. Instead he is patient with you, not wanting anyone to perish, but everyone to come to repentance" (2 Peter 3:9). God delays "the day of the LORD" because He is compassionate toward the sinner, and Christians must act upon His compassion by reaching out to the nations with the good news of Jesus Christ.

God chose the Jews to be His own special people, but God has also proven His love for the nations. He draws all people unto Himself. God said, "'It is too small a thing for you to be my servant to restore the tribes of Jacob and bring back those of Israel I have kept. I will also make you a light for the Gentiles, that my salvation may reach to the ends of the earth'" (Isaiah 49:6). The measure of His love compelled Him to send His own Son to be our Savior (John 3:16). God demonstrated this love at the cross, that "while we were still sinners, Christ died for us" (Romans 5:8).

Do you love the nations? Do you long to see the tribes, tongues, and nations worshipping God in heaven? Anger, fear, and selfishness can tempt Christians to care too little about the lost of the world. Haven't many of the lost people groups of the world declared themselves enemies of the LORD God? Don't many of them persecute Christians, hate Israel, and worship false gods? Aren't they deserving of God's wrath? Yes . . . and so am I, and so are you. We have all fallen short of God's glory, and the penalty we deserve is the full measure of God's wrath (Romans 3:23, 6:23). Aren't you grateful for God's gift of grace at the Cross? Praise God! God compels us to go into all the world to make disciples of the nations (Matthew 28:18–20).

Let us take the vision of Obadiah as a grave warning against taking any pleasure in the destruction of others. We'll leave the justice and judgment to God's courtroom. May we be joyful over our deliverance, and hopeful for the deliverance of all nations.

> *Prayer: Precious Lord, in my days of shame, You are my Restoration. When others try to bring me harm, You are my Deliverer. I praise You for Your guidance, even for those times when You have allowed me to learn from the consequences of*

my sin. May I never boast in the fall of others. Deliver even my enemies, God! Help me be a witness to the world. Help me overcome my own biases. You are the righteous Judge. Lord, save the nations, and use me for Your glory! Amen.

JOURNAL FOR THE MAJORS IN MY LIFE:

CHAPTER 5

Jonah: Complaining Prophet

by Kimberly Sowell

"You are a gracious and compassionate God, slow to anger and abounding in love, a God who relents from sending calamity." JONAH 4:2

J'm relieved to know I'm not the only person in the world who has terrible, panic-filled dreams about bad guys chasing me. I've experienced such motley characters as villains from movies, relatives gone bad, and even members of a rock band pursuing me in vivid nightmares, and my body wouldn't respond to help me get away. In these dreams, I grasp at my neck in desperation, but no sound comes from my mouth to let me cry for help. All of my will is set on escape, but my legs refuse to obey. The feelings of helplessness are overwhelming, and I wake up feeling terrified.

What are you running from these days? Maybe giant slabs of chocolate cake are chasing you in your dreams, or perhaps you're experiencing the reality of a nightmarish chase in real life. The prophet Jonah was also on the run, but the One pursuing him was the One who loved Jonah and had a great plan for his life. Jonah was running from the will of God.

MAN OVERBOARD (JONAH 1–2)

Willful disobedience — plain and simple, Jonah was willfully defying God's plan. God wanted Jonah to be His voice to Nineveh, a wicked, cruel people, and Jonah packed his belongings and ran the other way. Jonah was willing to pay a price — a ship fare for his journey — but little did he know a higher price was yet to come.

The majority of people walking about the earth are acutely unaware of God's existence and His interest in their lives. Many ignore God completely and act as though no higher authority exists beyond themselves. Others have a sense of a deity, but their pursuit of this "god" is trite and grossly falls short of the honor and glory befitting the King of kings. And Jonah? He was fully aware of the great I AM, but he underestimated the length of God's arms. Who can escape the presence of God? Who can hide his sin, or cause God to lose sight of him? The psalmist wrote, "Where can I go from Your Spirit? Or where can I flee from Your presence" (Psalm 139:7 NKJV)? The psalmist knew God's eyes see and His arms extend into infinity. Like the Psalmist, Jonah would learn in a very real way that "if I . . . .dwell in the uttermost parts of the sea, even there Your hand shall lead me, and Your right hand shall hold me" (Psalm 139:9–10 NKJV).

Every life tells a story, and Jonah's actions were communicating to the mariners a backwards message about the sovereignty of God. The mariners discovered God's authority over nature and His supremacy in the lives of His people through Jonah, but they were learning these lessons by watching God deal with Jonah with a strong hand. The mariners feared God as a result of this first close encounter with God, and even offered a sacrifice to Him (1:16). How gracious is our God! Even while God was working in a primary fashion in the life of Jonah, He was working in a secondary way to make the mariners aware of His identity. What irony that the mariners feared the God they had just met and cried out to Him for deliverance (1:14), while Jonah already had a knowledge of God and yet did not fear Him enough to obey.

As the waves crashed over Jonah's body, imagine the thoughts and emotions that must have also washed over his soul. If he thought his life was coming to a tragic end, he was woefully mistaken, because God had already prepared a fish to swallow Jonah. God could have used a limitless number of miraculous means to preserve Jonah's life, but He chose a rather exotic and probably unpleasant experience for Jonah. The belly of a fish was likely one smelly, disgusting timeout spot for Jonah to be still and think about who God is.

The three days and three nights spent in the fish was time well spent for Jonah. He came to some profound revelations about God. Jonah's poem of prayer in chapter two indicates that Jonah felt consumed and afraid as he sank into the depths of the sea, and he cried out to God. The experience of desperation that led to Jonah's dependence on God was the same experience the people of Nineveh needed in order to jolt them into action to cry out to God for forgiveness and help.

> **FAST FACT**
> Nineveh was built by Nimrod, son of Cush, son of Ham, son of Noah (Gen. 10:1-11). Nineveh was a capital city of the Assyrian Empire.

$\mathcal{M}$AJORING ON THE MINOR PROPHET

1. How did Jonah's disobedience bring anxiety and suffering to the mariners? Has another person's sin ever caused anxiety in your life?

2. What role did the mariners play in exposing Jonah's sin? How has God used people in your life who aren't Christians to help you grow spiritually?

3. Read Jonah's declaration in Jonah 1:9. Write your personal version of a one-sentence testimony of who you are and who God is in your life. Would you prefer to share this one-sentence testimony to unbelievers after they've observed you honoring God, or when you've disobeyed God, as Jonah did?

4. The mariners' first response to the great tempest was to cry out to their false gods. People often turn to the first thing they know when they're desperate and afraid. How would you word your testimony of God's power and love to an unbeliever who is afraid and in need of God's help?

5. Before the mariners threw Jonah overboard, they were willing to try to save themselves and Jonah by fighting the sea. Have you ever sought deliverance from a situation by trying to work it out yourself? What were the results?

6. How did God do a great work in the mariners' lives as a result of Jonah's disobedience? How does Proverbs 9:10 aptly describe what happened in the mariners' hearts? What is God saying to you about the many layers of His work in your life?

7. Once Jonah humbled himself, he gave thanks to God from inside the fish. Read 1 Thessalonians 5:18. Why is it possible to praise God and give thanks in the midst of a terrible circumstance?

U SE YOUR IMAGINATION

Like Jonah, have you ever fallen into what felt like a pit, a prison, or the belly of a big fish? Look carefully at Jonah's prayer in chapter 2. Write your own prayer poem about the experience you had of crying out to God from the pit. (If you have never had such an experience, use your imagination.) Try to include the many truth points that Jonah declared in his prayer:

- God will answer when we cry out (v. 2).
- Sin separates us from God (v. 3).
- In troubled times, we can look to the Lord (v. 4).
- Spiritual darkness is consuming (vv. 5–6).
- Painful, anxious moments can be tools to point us back to God (v. 7).
- Turning to anyone but God is useless (v. 8).
- In trials, we can give thanks, obey, and seek salvation in God alone (v. 9).

ROUND TWO (JONAH 3)

God spoke to Jonah a second time. We serve a God of second chances, and Jonah was ready to seize the opportunity to right his previous wrongs. Because of the smells and sensations Jonah experienced in the belly of the fish, Jonah may have had to go to extensive lengths in order to get cleaned up for the journey to Nineveh.

Unlike Jonah, the people of Nineveh were ready to respond to the word of the Lord the first time. They believed God and took swift action — fasting, humbling themselves before God, and repenting. Jonah may have felt a tinge of remorse and shame as he watched the nation of Nineveh falling to her knees in repentance, knowing he had not been so obedient to the Lord the first time God called him to Nineveh. What a humbling lesson to learn for the prophet of God.

Note the leadership of Nineveh's king. He led by example when he laid aside his royal robe and traded his splendor for humility. He called his people to prayer and instructed them to show great remorse for their sins. The king did not presume upon God; he gave no guarantee to the nation that God would turn away His holy wrath. However, the king encouraged his people to place their hope in the merciful nature of God. The king would not be disappointed.

$\mathcal{M}$AJORING ON THE MINOR PROPHET

1. What was the word of warning that Jonah was to deliver (3:4)?

2. Has God ever asked you to be His spokesperson? Before you answer, read and consider Acts 1:8.

3. Why did the people of Nineveh respond so swiftly (3:5)?

Some religious groups believe that inflicting pain upon themselves is necessary to please God. In 1999, the **Basilica of Our Lady of Guadalupe** became the most visited Catholic shrine in the world. **Many** pilgrims crawl on bloodied knees for miles as they approach the shrine, believing they will receive healing from their sicknesses.

4. Compare and contrast the actions and attitudes of the king of Nineveh and Jonah.

5. Carefully examine the marks of repentance in the people of Nineveh. What is the evidence of daily repentance in your life? How do you express to God that you take your sin seriously?

6. What has God promised about repentance in Isaiah 55:7?

*U*SE YOUR IMAGINATION

God sent a warning to Nineveh and expressed His displeasure over the people's sin. If tragedy would befall them, there was going to be no doubt the trouble was God's response to their disobedience. Sometimes when we experience troubles in our lives, we wrestle to discover if the problems are a result of living in this fallen world, a spiritual attack, the result of someone else's sin, or the direct result of our own sin. The next time you face a personal struggle, would you prefer for God to tell you directly the cause of the problem? Why or why not?

LESSONS YET LEARNED (JONAH 4)

Jonah was blind to his own sin. He was angry that God was "'slow to anger and abounding in love'" (4:2) toward the people of Nineveh, yet he failed to realize that he had also been a grand recipient of God's mercy and love throughout this entire process. God had worked in the lives of the mariners who were as gracious as possible to Jonah. Then God had prepared a fish to swallow Jonah, and by God's providence the experience didn't injure Jonah. At the appropriate time, the fish spit Jonah out at the right location so as not to cause Jonah to drown trying to get to shore. And once Jonah had finally obeyed God by travelling to Nineveh, God relented from striking Jonah down even though he was talking back to God! The story's scenes do not describe some of Jonah's finer moments.

Jonah took the status of Nineveh very personally. He wanted them to be punished for their sins and preferred they die, not prosper. He stationed himself on the east side of Nineveh to watch events unfold, wanting to learn of Nineveh's fate. How could Jonah have such a deep hatred for this people? Such depths of malice come from layers upon layers of anger that build up over time. As we study God's Word and learn about men and women of God who did great things for God's kingdom, we are sometimes tempted to place these matriarchs and patriarchs of the faith on a pedestal. Jonah's failures and personal frailties remind us that all of us have sinned and fallen short of God's glory (Rom. 3:23). Despite our sin, God is willing to use us to spread His message and proclaim His name to the nations. God uses the messenger to reach people with the truth, while God simultaneously molds and strengthens the heart of the messenger. The next time God calls you to service and Satan starts whispering in your ear about your weaknesses, remember that God can do incredible tasks through you for His glory. Don't run from the opportunity; joyfully obey!

MAJORING ON THE MINOR PROPHET

1. Read Jonah 4:2. List people for whom you are glad to experience God's lovingkindness. Now think about God's grace extended to your enemies (personal enemies, or people groups who may despise you as a Christian.) Can you say with an honest heart that you long for your enemies to experience God's grace?

2. Consider God's question in Jonah 4:4. What have you been angry about lately? List those situations below. Then answer God's question in Jonah 4:4 for yourself.

3. Read Matthew 18:21–35. Have you fully forgiven the people in your life? Can you freely seek their wellbeing?

4. When God gave Jonah the shade plant to sit beneath for a day, how was God showing patience with Jonah? How was his time spent in the fish similar to this time under the shade plant? Has God ever given you "time out" to think and come to your senses?

5. Why did Jonah value the plant more than the people of Jonah?

6. Jonah is in some ways an archetype of Jesus. Beside each point below, write how Jesus had a *similar* or *opposite* experience or calling.

   • Jonah was told by God to call Nineveh to repentance. (Hint: see Matthew 4:17.)

   • Jonah was not obedient to God.

   • During the storm, Jonah was asleep. (Hint: see Matthew 8:24.)

- Jonah was the cause of the turmoil of the sea. (Hint: see Matthew 8:26.)

- Jonah spent three days and nights in the belly of the fish.

- Jonah was angry that the people were spared God's wrath.

7. Jonah's anger was extended to God, because God Himself was delivering peace to Nineveh. Do you expect your friends or even God to "take your side" when you are upset with someone?

8. How did Jonah rob himself from joy in service? Are you indulging an attitude that is robbing you of experiencing the fullness of joy that comes in serving the Lord?

$\mathcal{U}$ SE YOUR IMAGINATION

Carefully examine Jonah 4:10–11. Notice God's compassion for Nineveh and His attention to the details of the people. Now think of a country on the planet whose people have rejected Jesus Christ and His gift of salvation. What would God have to say to you to convince you to join Him in showing mercy and kindness to the people of this nation? What are some creative ways you could show God's love to them? How could you share God's message with them?

$\mathcal{F}$ URTHER REFLECTIONS

The Book of Jonah is about people's shortcomings and God's patience. God was patient and merciful to the sinners of Nineveh, and He was equally patient and merciful to Jonah. Examine God's Word to discover other stories that display God's patience and mercy. How does God's plan of salvation through Jesus Christ display His patience and mercy for the world?

Allow the lessons of Jonah to help you have the right attitude the next time someone wrongs you. Rather than reacting in anger, respond with patience and mercy. Jot down thoughts of how God has shown patience and mercy to you, and ask God to help you tell your offender that you can forgive him or her because of what God has done in your life.

Prayer: Precious Lord, I also have been guilty of not always seeking the wellbeing of others. Whether my lack of love was expressed in silence or a willful rejection of Your calling to share love and truth with my enemies, please forgive me. Please teach me to be an agent of Your peace. God, give me a desire to be swift in my obedience to You, never demanding my way or questioning Your authority. Amen.

$\mathcal{J}$OURNAL FOR THE MAJORS IN MY LIFE:

CHAPTER 6

Micah: Conscience of the Nation

by Tricia Scribner

He has showed you, O man, what is good. And what does the LORD require of you? To act justly and to love mercy and to walk humbly with your God. MICAH 6:8

J have been astonished in recent years at the apparent success of preachers who fill thousands of seats within their churches simply by telling people what they want to hear. Their messages of prosperity and health may please the people who flock to hear them, but they do not represent the true message of God. There can be no true spiritual prosperity or health without confession of sin and repentance.

Micah in his time found that his messages were resisted by the people who most needed to hear the truth about their sin. They wanted to hear about God's mercy rather than His justice, preferring self-deception to the truth that their sin had broken fellowship with God and resulted in terrible consequences that would eventually destroy their nation.

Micah was a contemporary of Isaiah who preached in Judah and of Hosea who prophesied in Israel. His ministry covered the last third of the eighth century about 730 B.C. His messages addressed both Judah and Israel, with

BEWARE OF THE HIGH PLACES

The patriarchs such as Abraham often built altars on tops of mountains or hills to offer sacrifices to the LORD (Genesis 12:7-8). But when the Israelites entered the Promised Land, God commanded them to purge the land of all high places because the pagan people who lived there worshipped idols in these specially designed locations, decorating them with altars, sacred pillars, and carved wooden images of idols (Deuteronomy 12:2-3). At some points, the Israelites mixed their worship of the LORD with the worship of false gods at the high places, treating the one, true God as just another of their idolatrous pantheon. So, God instructed them that, unlike the pagan locals, His people, the Israelites, were to worship Him only in places that He chose (Deuteronomy 12:5). Unfortunately, despite God's warning not to continue to

a focus on Judah. Further, his words echoed those of Amos who had preached against similar sins in Israel shortly before Micah's ministry began.

The book can be divided into three main sections (chaps. 1–2, 3–5, 6–7), each section rotating between a message of judgment and a message of restoration.

A TRUTH THAT HURTS AND HELPS (MICAH 1:1 TO 2:13)

In Micah 1:1–7 the prophet called all the earth's nations to hear the Lord's evidence against His people. Metaphorically God was portrayed as leaving His heavenly abode and entering earth's scene to execute judgment. He trampled the high places of pagan worship underfoot, melted the mountains like wax, and split the valleys, so great was His power.

Micah laid blame for the fall of both kingdoms squarely upon the citizens of each one's capital city: Samaria for northern Israel and Jerusalem for southern Judah. In fact, he claimed that the capital cities were the epitomes of evil. Samaria

do what was right in their own eyes but instead to obey the Lord (Deut. 12:8-9), the Israelites continued to tolerate and then to embrace the idol worship that took place in the high places until the time of exile (1 Kings 13:32; 2 Kings 14:4 to 17:29).

was the very "transgression" of Israel and Jerusalem was the "high place" of Judah (v. 5).

In 1:8–16, when Micah realized the attacks would eventually bring down not only the Northern Kingdom but also the cities of the Southern Kingdom, he was overcome with grief and responded with a lament, a formal expression of mourning. He described his soul-wrenching sorrow graphically, including weeping, wailing, going naked and barefoot, and howling and moaning.

Returning to his initial theme of sin in the land, in chapter 2:1–5 Micah presented his judgment against evil that the people had committed. Specifically, he accused them of premeditating evil on their beds at night and then defrauding landowners, stealing their land. As a result the land would be divided, the allotments not going to God's people as God had originally planned, but to foreign invaders.

Micah's message was not well received. In fact, in 2:6–11 the false prophets in the land completely rejected Micah's words of warning, insisting that instead God was going to bless

HOW GREAT WAS THE FALL OF IT

Assyria's Shalmaneser V (followed by his successor Sargon II) attacked Samaria in 722/721 B.C., taking many people of Israel away to Assyria. Assyria continued its attacks through the reign of Sennacherib who razed the land all the way to Jerusalem's gates in 701 B.C. during the reign of Judah's King Hezekiah. Sennacherib tried to intimidate Hezekiah into surrendering. Due to Hezekiah's repentance, God spared Judah for a time (2 Kings 19). Jerusalem finally fell in 587/586 B.C. to the new superpower, Babylon's Nebuchadnezzar.

them. Despite widespread thievery of women's and children's homes, they saw no incongruence between their incurable spiritual disease and their expectation of blessing.

Suddenly, in 2:12–13 Micah's message shifted to a future time beyond the devastation to reveal that Messiah as the Shepherd would one day save His people. The Lord's own words announced that He would gather the remnant like sheep. This was likely a reference that reflected a time beyond the return of the exiles, into the millennial reign when Messiah would "go up before them" and "their king will pass through before them, the LORD at their head" (v. 13). Isn't it just like our God to instill hope in the face of our failures? If only the people had listened, their sins would have been forgiven, their relationship with God restored, and their land once again prosperous.

MAJORING ON THE MINOR PROPHET

1. What do you think kept the people from accepting Micah's messages of rebuke?

2. How did the people see themselves in relationship to God?

3. What does their response tell us about human nature?

4. Why is the message of 2:12–13 so significant on the heels of Micah's rebuke?

U SE YOUR IMAGINATION

1. Think of a time you had trouble receiving a true but painful message. What was that like for you? How did you respond? If you could go back, would you respond differently? How so?

2. When we have failed and someone confronts us, we can respond in several ways, such as denial, anger, blaming, rationalization, and/or withdrawal. Instead of these destructive responses, God offers another option. Read 1 John 1:8–9. God offers complete forgiveness and cleansing from all our sin. We do not have to fear His rejection. In fact, Jesus Christ already paid the price for every sin we commit. For this reason, we can run humbly to the Savior's arms, agree with Him, and receive a clean slate.

GRACE GREATER THAN SIN (MICAH 3:1 TO 5:15)
In 3:1–12 Micah addressed the leaders of Israel directly. His verbal reprisal must have stung their hearts. He described the leaders of the nation as

haters of good and lovers of evil. The ones most educated in the character and execution of justice abused the people in horrible ways. Read his graphic description in 3:1–4. Micah expressed their injustice and abuse as a butchering and cannibalization of God's people.

Then, in verses 5–8 Micah, a prophet of God, spoke *against* the current set of prophets. With a complete disregard for truth, the messages of the nation's prophets hinged only on the highest bid, charged Micah. If paid well, they proclaimed peace. If paid poorly, they howled war. As prophets went, Micah stood in stark contrast to the usual proclaimers of peace. In verse 8, he divorced himself from their methods and their motivations, affirming that he himself was filled with power, the Spirit of the Lord, and with "justice and might." As a true messenger of God, he was bound to proclaim truth and thus "to declare to Jacob his transgression, to Israel his sin" rather than the syrupy lie of sweetness the false prophets proclaimed.

At the end of chapter 3, in verses 9–12, Micah summarized the sins of the nation's leaders and then issued a terrible proclamation. Because of their sin, cruelty, hatred of the God of truth, and because on top of their heinous crimes, they saw themselves as the apple of God's eye and therefore immune from punishment, their glorious temple mount would be destroyed and would waste away beneath the overgrowth of thickets.

If the book were to end with chapter 3, we might just sit down and cry. The picture is bleak and the story ends sadly. But one prominent feature of Micah is the rotating back and forth between themes of rebuke for sin and themes of salvation. So, just when we are tempted to weep, Micah breaks forth with the glorious promise of hope. In fact, the glory of chapters 4 and 5 put the failures of God's people into an eternal perspective and refocus on the magnificent truth that God's grace is always greater than our sin.

Read 4:1–8 and notice that no longer was Micah speaking solely of the Jewish people but also of the nations or "peoples" of the earth. And look at their destination: the holy city of Jerusalem. Now, remember that the previous chapter graphically portrayed a nation in ruins. But immediately following, here in chapter 4, he described the temple mount where the very presence of God dwelt in His house. Moreover, from this location God Himself would proclaim His law and the people would actually desire to follow Him! Verse 3 is one of the most well-known verses referring to the messianic kingdom, or millennial reign, to come. We know it has not yet occurred by the descriptions of the era, descriptions that are unique to a time when war will be no more, and people will live in peace without fear.

Though the future will bring ultimate peace, in the meantime Babylon awaited, according to verses 10–13. For God's people, circumstances would get worse before they got better. This turn of events was not accidental but part of God's plan. Unlike Micah, the people failed to grasp the big picture.

Chapter 5:1–6 contains the specific promise of the Ruler who would come from Bethlehem of Judah. But the promise would be fulfilled only after Israel was "abandoned" to its enemies. After that time was fulfilled, then the Shepherd Ruler would come. Verse 5 asserts that this Ruler would

Bethlehem of Ephrathah is located about five miles south of Jerusalem on a prominent hill. Ephrathah was an ancient name for the town or the district in which it was located. Genesis 35:19 recorded that Rachel died in childbirth on the road to Bethlehem. During the time of the judges, Ruth the Moabitess followed her mother-in-law Naomi to Bethlehem (Ruth 1:19), and there married Boaz, becoming King David's great-grandmother. During David's time the Philistines used the site as a garrison for their soldiers (2 Samuel 23:14), and David called it by its ancient name in Psalm 132:6. The town fell into obscurity until Micah mentioned its surprising destiny as the birthplace of Messiah (5:2). In the New Testament Matthew (2:6) quoted Micah's prophecy about Bethlehem as being fulfilled in the circumstances of Jesus Christ's birth. Bethlehem of Ephrathah is distinguished from another town called Bethlehem of Zebulun, located in northern Galilee, near Nazareth.

"be their peace," when enemies such as Assyria (a likely general reference to all enemies of God's people) invaded the land. Many scholars believe that this is a reference to the end time attack against Israel in which God will intervene to save His people. Israel will raise up "seven . . . eight leaders," a common Hebraic reference, to mean the country would mobilize plenty of leaders to stand victoriously in the crisis against Israel's enemies.

The next section, Micah 5:7–15, spoke of the remnant of God's people, dispersed among foreign nations, who would be the source of blessing but also a tool of God's judgment against their oppressors. Further, God would eradicate Israel's pagan worship and judge the nations who disobeyed Him, some of whom helped lead the nation of Israel into idolatry.

MAJORING ON THE MINOR PROPHET

1. Read Micah 3:8. How did Micah distinguish himself from the evil prophets of the nation?

2. List the types of pagan worship mentioned in 5:10–15. What does this passage say about the destiny of pagan worship in Israel? It is significant to note that after the return from exile, though God's people failed in many ways, the idol worship that had plagued the land dissipated.

*U*SE YOUR IMAGINATION

1. Read 2 Corinthians 2:14–1   6. Now read Micah 5:7–9. Notice in both passages God's people are dispersed among the nations, living among pagans. And in both passages God's people are both a blessing and tool of God's judgment to unbelievers. How have you noticed that your being a Christian is a blessing to unbelievers among whom you live and work? How is your presence a frustration or an offense to unbelievers?

2. Reading through 4:1–8 and 5:1–6, make a list of the changes enacted when the Ruler Messiah reigns. List reasons we can look forward to Messiah's millennial reign.

FAITHLESS NATION OF A FAITHFUL GOD (6:1 TO 7:20)

Whereas in the first section in chapter 1 God called the nations to listen to His evidence against His people, in the third section (starting in 6:1–2) He called forth the very mountains and hills to bear witness of his testimony against the nation. He demanded that His people answer Him, asking what He had done to warrant their faithlessness. He described in 6:3–5 how He had saved them out of Egypt and recounted the incident in which the prophet Balaam was supernaturally constrained by God to pronounce blessing upon Israel rather than the curse that Balak, king of Moab, demanded. Further, He protected them when they crossed over the Jordan into the land, traveling from their last stop east of the Jordan at Shittim to the west of the river in

Gilgal. Were these the actions that deserved such brazen rejection?

Finally, in verses 6–8, when the people rhetorically speculated on what they could do to please God such as bring sacrifices — maybe even their firstborn children — God emphatically restated what He had told them many times before, exactly what His righteous nature required of the people called by His own name. He did not want their sacrifices. Even the sacrifice of their firstborn could not earn a right relationship with God. Instead, God wanted them to take on the character of their God, revealed in their just actions and love of mercy toward others. He wanted them to exchange their arrogant self-sufficiency for a humble attitude toward Him.

As you read 6:9 to 7:6 notice how God described the evils among his people, including common cheating in the marketplace, abuses by the rich, habitual lying, violence, bribery, abuse of power, and disrespect of parents. The magnitude of sin justified God's bringing them to ruin.

In 7:7 Micah distinguished himself from those in rebellion against God. He waited expectantly for His God to intervene. As the final message of Micah closed in 7:8–20, Micah humbly placed himself and his nation in the hands of his righteous God. Sin had caused their fall but they trusted the Lord's deliverance and the downfall of their enemies. God would forgive their sin, and heal and restore their land.

MAJORING ON THE MINOR PROPHET

1. Read Psalm 51:17, comparing it with the commands of Micah 6:6–8. What actions do and do not comprise true worship in the eyes of God based on these passages?

2. What similarities do you see in the descriptions of Micah 6:14–15 and Haggai 1:6?

$\mathcal{U}$ SE YOUR IMAGINATION

1. As you read through Micah 6:9 to 7:6, what sins did Micah mention that you see in your own life?

2. Write a poem or psalm of trust in the Lord's forgiveness, goodness, and righteousness.

> *Prayer: Lord Jesus, I recognize that at times I have failed You without fear of discipline because I am Your loved child. Please forgive me and show me how to be holy as You are holy. Amen.*

JOURNAL FOR THE MAJORS IN MY LIFE:

CHAPTER 7

Nahum: Poetic Justice

by Tricia Scribner

The LORD is slow to anger and great in power; the LORD will not leave the guilty unpunished. NAHUM 1:3

Sometimes people who practice evil seem to flourish, oblivious to the depravity of their crimes. They prosper financially from sordid business dealings and sit ensconced in fine homes. It just doesn't seem fair. Of course, when it comes to my own wickedness, I believe God should know I didn't mean it and give me a do-over.

We know very little about the prophet Nahum. He may have written his book around 630ish B.C. since his writing seemed to speak of Nineveh's fall in future tense. We aren't sure the meaning of his name though it comes from the Hebrew root word meaning "to comfort." We don't even know for certain the location of his hometown, Lekosh. But what we do know is remarkable. Nahum's message was concise, radical—and at the same time—poetic in its form. God was about to take down the international superpower's seat of power, Nineveh. There was no remedy. The time for repentance had passed. Destruction was inevitable.

That Nineveh's destruction would be the primary source of comfort for the people of Judah seems vengeful to some. Some scholars have argued

WHERE WAS NINEVEH?
The city of Nineveh was located on the east side of the Tigris River across from the current city of Mosul, Iraq.

that the message of Nahum is incompatible with the character of a loving, forgiving, and merciful God. But God's mercy and love becomes pathetic indulgence in the absence of His justice. The prophet Jonah had witnessed the city's repentance after reluctantly preaching his dire warning against their evil ways some 100 to 150 years prior, but their change of heart was short-lived.

The Assyrians were well known for their cruelty. Their policy of exiling overrun nations tore the Northern Kingdom apart with the conquering of Samaria in 722/21 B.C. To add insult to injury, they had resettled the land with foreigners and run roughshod over everyone in their way.

Despite their self-confidence that seemed warranted by their numerous military conquests, Assyria, unknown to them, was about to take a mega-fall. Southern Judah's people, whom the Assyrians had delighted in harassing and humiliating long after the conquest of northern Samaria, were about to come face to face with a holy God, who is slow to anger, but whose justice is sure.

A HOLY GOD (NAHUM 1:1–15)

One of the most stunning features of Nahum's book is lost on English readers. Scholars have described Nahum as a sublime example of Hebrew poetry. We will look at several of these poetic features unique to Nahum as we study.

Nahum 1:1–3 describes God as jealous. When referring to God, jealousy is a righteous zeal that requires complete devotion and is a holy attribute. God will not take second place. Nahum also described Him as "slow to anger," a trait that reflected patience and long-suffering in God's dealings with mankind. God also, however, knows the human heart and when the heart is so hardened, it will never turn. Then comes judgment.

In 1:4–6 Nahum described the power of God's judgment in graphic terms. Bashan and Carmel were fertile Palestinian lands. God dried the sea of Exodus and the lush flora withered under his gaze. All natural forces, including earthquakes and landslides, are under His control.

This same God, said Nahum, in 1:7–11, the One whose power terrified, was the God who was the Refuge and Protector of those who loved and trusted Him. In verse 7 Nahum used antithetical parallelism, linking two lines by contrast. While He was a refuge in trouble for His own, He overwhelmed His enemies with a flood.

In 1:12–14 the enemy was completely destroyed, their names literally wiped off the face of the earth, along with their idols. Specifically, the Lord said three consequences of Nineveh's evil would come about: (1) God would blot out her name; (2) God would see to it that just as Assyria had confiscated all the idols from the temples her kings conquered, so would God plunder the idols and images from Assyria's temples; (3) God would prepare a burial place for Assyria, where her disgusting corpse would be placed.

CHARACTERISTICS OF HEBREW POETRY

One-third of the Old Testament is poetry. Whereas a prominent feature of English poetry is rhyme, ancient Hebrew poetry used other literary devices such as parallelism and the acrostic. In Hebrew, for instance, Nahum 1:2-8 was written as an acrostic, employing a sequential lineup of the letters of the Hebrew alphabet. In Nahum 1:6, the prophet used synonymous parallelism, in which the thought of the first line paralleled the thought of the second line by repeating the same idea using different but synonymous words; for example: Line 1: "Who can withstand his indignation?" Line 2: "Who can endure his fierce anger?" These literary devices enabled an oral culture to commit to memory lengthy stories and the history of their nation that God had commanded them to pass on from one generation to the next.

Finally, in 1:15 Nahum explained the purpose of his writing. The God who protected His chosen ones was enacting His plan to demonstrate that protection. This verse had other immediate and long-term implications. The imminent destruction of Assyria foreshadowed a future universal destruction of Judah's enemies and a time when peace would reign. Notice the similarity in wording of Nahum 1:15 and Isaiah 52:7, which says, "How beautiful on the mountains are the feet of those who bring good news, who proclaim peace, who bring good tidings, who proclaim salvation, who say to Zion, 'Your God reigns!'" Isaiah's passage prophesied the return of the exiles from Babylon, whereas Nahum announced his message to encourage Judah that the rule of Assyria would end and the restoration of Judah's yearly observances of holy days could be reinstituted.

*M*AJORING ON THE MINOR PROPHET

1. The idea that the Lord was slow to anger but does not leave the guilty unpunished is a theme in Nahum. Read Exodus 34:6–7. Describe the circumstances in which God spoke words similar to Nahum 1:3. How was the Exodus proclamation similar? How do the wordings differ?

2. Read Jonah 3:10 to 4:2. Why do you think the Jonah passage describes God's character as gracious, compassionate, and slow to anger but does not mention the surety of His punishment of the wicked as in Nahum 1:3?

3. Jonah and Nahum hold several characteristics in common. They were the only two Old Testament books written solely about Nineveh. Both books also close with questions. Jonah 4:11: "And should I not have concern for the great city of Nineveh, in which there are more than a hundred and twenty thousand people who cannot tell their right hand from their left — and also many animals?" In Nahum: "All who hear the news about you clap their hands at your fall, for who has not felt your endless cruelty?" But the differences in these questions are marked. In Jonah, God rebuked Jonah's desire to invoke God's wrath on Nineveh's people. In contrast, in Nahum the prophet rejoiced over the fall of Nineveh. How do we account for the difference in God's attitude and actions regarding Nineveh during Jonah's time as compared to Nahum's? Reread Jonah 3:5–10, noting the people's response to God's message during Jonah's time. God has always recognized human repentance and restored relationship on that basis. But Nineveh's repentance was short-lived.

U SE YOUR IMAGINATION

1. To what degree would your family say you are slow to anger?

2. How often is your anger like God's righteous anger against evil against God's righteousness rather than due to offenses against you?

3. How does Nahum 1:15 demonstrate God's care for the weak, abused, and helpless? Recall a time when you were suffering that God showed His love for you.

A BULLY BROUGHT DOWN (NAHUM 2:1-13)

I remember the day in December 2003 when reporters announced the capture of Saddam Hussein, who had terrorized the people of Iraq for more than 30 years. When he was finally caught while hiding in a cellar of a farmhouse in the town of Adwar, I prayed for his repentance. But like many people throughout the world, there was a sense of relief that this despot had been brought down. Nahum announced to Judah that the bully on their street, Assyria with its capital Nineveh, was about to be defeated. The words Nahum proclaimed to Nineveh were not actually read by the Ninevites initially but by Judah's people, and they brought rejoicing.

Read Nahum 2:1-2. To the same degree that Nineveh would be defeated, Judah would be exalted. The splendor of Nineveh would soon be destroyed while the splendor of Judah would be restored to its former glory. Though an ultimate restoration of Judah would one day eclipse all others, the land was significantly restored when good king Josiah ascended Judah's throne in 627 B.C. and about the same time Assyria's king, Ashurbanipal, died.

In verses 3-5 Nahum described the city's attackers rushing in with chariot metal clanking and glinting in the sun. Notice Nahum's vivid portrayal of the attack. Finally, in verses 6–10, Nineveh's citizens, terrorized and disoriented, watched in horror as their treasures were plundered and the people captured and taken away as prisoners of war. Nahum then employed a metaphor in verses 11–12 describing Assyria, the self-proclaimed lion of the empire, shamed. The lion's den, once filled with the prey of successful hunts like a lion bringing his kills to its cave, was no more. In verse 13 God took His stand against them. The shining chariots would burn and the smoke of their burning would billow. The sword would strike down their young and deathly silence would hang like a pall throughout the land.

Assyria's Ashurbanipal bragged about his cruel treatment of his conquered enemies. He claimed to have severed the tongues of those who had blasphemed his god and plotted against him, the god's prince. He claimed to have crushed alive other enemies, and then cut up their corpses and fed them to pigs and dogs. He also claimed to have made soldiers stand guard by water-filled cisterns from which he would not permit them to drink, just to torture them and watch them die slowly in agony. He bragged that other soldiers were forced to cut open camels to get whatever liquid they could salvage to save their lives. It was against this kind of heinous cruelty and disregard for human life that Nahum spoke God's verdict of final punishment and His people rightly rejoiced.

MAJORING ON THE MINOR PROPHET

1. According to Nahum 2:3–4, 7, 9, 13, how would the Assyrians suffer a similar fate as those nations who had previously fallen at Assyria's hands?

2. Describe the terror an individual would feel during the attack, according to Nahum 2:10.

3. What does Nahum 2:13 reveal about the power of God's certainty and scope of God's wrath?

$\mathcal{U}$ SE YOUR IMAGINATION

1. Can you think of an evil international figure at whose fall you rejoiced; similar to how the people of Judah may have rejoiced at the prospect of Assyria's fall?

2. How can we rejoice at the fall of evil powers without having a vengeful spirit?

HE WHO LIVES BY THE SWORD (NAHUM 3:1-19)

Many Hollywood icons seem to view themselves as above the law as they say and do things flagrantly immoral and often illegal. Similarly, Assyria's Nineveh saw itself as immune from prosecution by a holy God.

The next section of 3:1–7 mocks God's enemies, in this case Nineveh, in a declaration of joy at the demise of the wicked. The city's leaders had stockpiled the wealth looted from conquered nations. Nahum described their enemy's attack on them in short abrupt bursts. The dead would pile up in the streets. The reasons for this horror, Nahum said, was their harlotry. They had lured other nations into their trap evidently through demonic practices such as witchcraft. Ancient Assyrian writings testify to the common practices of astrology, the seeking of omens, and other magical arts.

Egypt's *Thebes* (a name assigned by the Greeks but which the Egyptians called *Waset*) is now called *Luxor*, located about 400 miles south of the city of Cairo. For nearly 2000 years the city sat untouched by outside powers, until its fall to Assyria about 663 B.C. It once served as the home of a great temple dedicated to the worship of the sun god Amun-Re and thus was called the "City of Amun." Thebes is also mentioned in Jeremiah 46:25 and in Ezekiel 30:14-16.

God so despised Assyria's idolatry and mocking of the one, true God, He would "lift your skirts over your face" (v. 5), a reference to the humiliating punishment for prostitutes. Her nakedness would be exposed to the world. In addition, God would heap filth upon her, and the nations would look upon her death without remorse or mourning.

Did the people of Nineveh think they were invincible? Evidently so. They had won so many battles, conquered so many nations, and plundered so many national treasures that they had begun to believe their own press. They flaunted their brutality with pride.

In verses 8–11 Nahum reminded the readers of the fall of the great city of

Thebes. The Ninevites should have learned from the fall of Thebes to Assyria's own Ashurbanipal that no city was invincible. Like Nineveh, Assyria's capital on the Tigris River, Thebes had been Egypt's capital city strategically positioned on the Nile. Also like Nineveh Thebes believed its access to the Nile assured its security. Though she had courted two allies, Put (Ethiopia) and Libya, Thebes still fell. Her babies were mercilessly butchered and her nobles sold to the highest bidder. Such would be Nineveh's end, as well.

Nahum's words in verses 12–18 portray metaphorically Nineveh's seemingly formidable defenses as ripe fruit, ready for the picking. In fact, it was literally falling from the vine into the mouths of those waiting. Instead of the muscled strength of men, the Ninevites were as weak as women. Instead of their gates shielding the city, they were flung open, exposing the city to its attackers. Nahum mockingly urged Nineveh to try to protect herself, but no matter how great the effort, the defense was hopeless. Nahum closed his book with an epitaph. The city's wound was fatal; her demise applauded. Like all of God's enemies, her destruction was sure and complete.

$\mathcal{M}$AJORING ON THE MINOR PROPHET

1. Nahum's book is filled with vivid poetry. Write an epitaph or a poem about the fall of Nineveh and praising the all-powerful God who executes judgment against His enemies.

2. List the similarities between Thebes and Nineveh. Why do you think the Ninevites did not recognize those similarities?

3. Jonah preached to Nineveh about a century earlier and they repented. Why do you think they returned to old evil patterns of thinking and behavior?

U SE YOUR IMAGINATION

1. Read Matthew 5:44–48. Some readers see a contradiction in Nahum's rejoicing at the fall of Judah's enemy in light of God's command for us to love and forgive our enemies. What do you think and why?

2. In what which ways does Nineveh's wicked arrogance remind you of America? If you were to preach a message to this country, what would you say to warn against a similar fate as that of Nineveh?

Prayer: Lord, thank You that though we all are wicked, Your mercy secures the future of those who humble themselves before you. I praise You for Your fair and righteous judgment of those who reject You and that in the end, evil will not win. May I learn from the fall of the arrogant that I, too, will face the Holy, Righteous Judge of the earth.

JOURNAL ON THE MAJORS IN MY LIFE:

CHAPTER 8

Habakkuk: Joyful Singer

by Edna Ellison

I will rejoice in the Lord, I will be joyful in God my Savior.
HABAKKUK. 3:18

I spent one beautiful night in Panama City that changed my life. On a missions trip, we spent 24 hours in a nice hotel in the city before going to the mission site. As the sun went down, I lay in bed looking out the wide panorama windows at the ships lined up to go through the locks of the Panama Canal. For the first time, I saw flags of all nations in proximity, as a variety of large and small ships slowly moved through the gates. I watched people in Arab turbans and another group in baseball caps just a few feet from each other, waving from ship to ship, experiencing the same journey, joined in a common moment. God brought to my mind the prayer I had memorized as a child: "May the peoples praise you, O God; may all the peoples praise you. May the nations be glad and sing for joy, for you rule the peoples justly and guide the nations of the earth" (Psalm 67:3–4). As stars began to shine above these ships, I thought of God's guiding them through the night to far destinations and His blessings on all nations around the world. Since that night, I've been more mindful of our small world and how we interrelate with

BACKGROUND

The name Habakkuk is a derivative of a Hebrew word which means "to clasp" or "to embrace." Because passages in Habakkuk refer to musical directions, we may assume he was a cantor, musical conductor, or choir director. A contemporary of Jeremiah (who ministered from 626 B.C. to after 586 B.C.), Habakkuk had vigorous faith, steeped in the religious traditions of Israel. Bible scholars have dated the Book of Habakkuk around 605 B.C. This prophecy, or "oracle" as it is called in verse 1, was recorded around the time of the battle of Carchemish. [For more information on the two defeats at Carchemish (sometimes spelled *Charchemish*), a town on the Euphrates River, read 2 Chronicles 35:20-25, Jeremiah 46:2, and Isaiah 10:9.]

others. With God's guidance through the tight places of life and on to calmer seas, we have Someone to sing about!

The most-quoted verse I hear often from Habakkuk is, "Look at the nations and watch — and be utterly amazed. For I am going to do something in your days that you would not believe, even if you were told" (1:5). This one optimistic verse assures us that God is moving in our world today. It points us to all nations as we watch Him move among us. It encourages us to stand in amazement at what He is doing in our world, and it describes our incredible awe as we respond to His power. However, we need to consider not just this popular verse from Habakkuk, but the surrounding verses. Today, ask for God's wisdom as you read the three short chapters of Habakkuk.

HABAKKUK: MUSICAL COMPLAINER (HABAKKUK 1:1–17)

Habakkuk opens his discourse with a complaint against God (vv. 1–4), highlighted by these key words: *long, call,* and *listen*. Pause over each of these words as you imagine a prophet asking God "How long must I call for help and you do not listen?" We can sympathize with Habakkuk because

This Old Testament book is a dialogue between God and Habakkuk. It begins with Habakkuk's complaints, presents God's response, and then records another complaint on the method God is using to turn His people away from haughty complacency and decadence to righteousness and humility. It ends with Habakkuk's song of praise for the Lord, no matter what the circumstances.

we often complain to our Lord. We complain the loudest when we have to wait for an answer or a clear response from God. We know too well that even a short time of waiting seems lengthy. Rewording this lament, Habakkuk cries out "Violence" (or "Help! Murder! Police" *The Message*).

After complaining about God's inattention and refusal to help him, Habakkuk brings up the issues that bother him (v. 3): God's toleration of injustice, making him live with destruction, and placing him in a violent area. He also brings up the subject of ineffective law enforcement and injustice in the civil court system; it's obvious to him that wicked people take advantage of poor righteous people who are suffering.

God responds in full force, with one of the most shocking passages in the Old Testament. Read verse 5 again. Notice that He asks Habakkuk to do two things: (1) look at the nations, and (2) be utterly amazed. He then gives Habakkuk a promise: "I am going to do something in your days that you would not believe even if you were told." Most Christians think these words are positive, that God is going to perform mighty miracles for His people. In a world of terror, corruption, and danger, God is still in control. However, as you read the next verses, you may think they are extremely negative. God is going to use foreign agents, the Babylonians, to wipe the slate clean. In the next few verses (6–11), Habakkuk gives a description of the Babylonians and the terrible behaviors he has seen in them. As you read each one, note in the margin or in today's journal how that behavior still exists in your world. Then read verses 12–17; can you identify with the heartfelt words of Habakkuk?

Who do you believe are the "sea creatures that have no ruler"?

*M*AJORING ON THE MINOR PROPHET

1. Read Jeremiah 14:8, comparing Jeremiah's complaints to those of Habakkuk. How does Habakkuk imply that God is a transient, not trustworthy for a longtime relationship?

2. Have you ever complained to God in similar ways or cried out, "How long must I wait?" When?

BAD GUYS OF THE BIBLE: THE BABYLONIAN EMPIRE

The city-state of Babylon (present-day Baghdad) rose after the fall of the Third Dynasty of Ur, which had ruled the cities in Mesopotamia's fertile plains between the Euphrates and Tigris Rivers (present-day Iraq) in the 2100s–2000s B.C. The Amorite kings, conquering the region, reigned as the First Dynasty of Babylon from approximately 1894–1595 B.C. After that, warring tribes spent decades capturing and recapturing a statue of Marduk, a popular pagan idol in the region. This period, known as the "Middle Babylonian Period," accepted another group of settlers, the Chaldaeans, who blended into the Babylonian culture. In the Bible, Babylonians are sometimes called "Chaldaeans" interchangeably. After this era of transition, the Assyrians conquered the region (883–859), but Babylonia claimed its independence in the 700s B.C.

3. Compare Habbakuk 1:16 to Isaiah 22:13 and Luke 12:19, 34. How do these words remind you of excesses in your world?

3. Name some repulsive habits of the Babylonians you see in today's world.

4. In which of the following ways will you change the world? *(a)* Protest in the streets; *(b)* Pray for peace; *(c)* Write your congress representative; *(d)* Help at local soup kitchens; *(e)* Be an advocate for a poor person; *(f)* Trust God to be sovereign.

In the years when Habakkuk was prophesying, a former Assyrian soldier, Nabopolassar, declared himself king of Babylon. After he was recognized as king on November 23, 626 B.C., he secured peace for the region through treaties with the Assyrians and the nearby Medes. Later he arranged a marriage with his son, crown prince Nebuchadnezzar, to a Mede princess, Amytis.

King Josiah of Judah, an ancestor of Jesus (Matthew 1:10-11), tried to resist the Assyrians, but they allied with Egyptians for a battle victory, in which Josiah was killed at Megiddo (2 Chronicles 35:20-24). In 605, Nebuchadnezzar killed the Egyptian pharaoh, Necho, near Charchemish, on the banks of the Euphrates River.

5. Do the behaviors Habakkuk lists in verses 6–11 still exist today?

   If so, who do you think is guilty of terror? Where?

6. *Why* do you believe terror still exists in the world?

7. Record how you feel about such injustice.

STANDING WATCH ON THE WALL

In chapters 1 and 2, Habakkuk's words are filled with shock and awe. He cannot believe the loving God he knows will use the Babylonians to punish His own people! What had God's people done to deserve this? The NIV Committee on Bible Translation (International Bible Society, 1978) says that Habakkuk and "the people of God were caught up in a crisis of religious and moral bewilderment." When you think of common life in your community, you may feel your neighbors or even your family is in a crisis of religious and moral confusion. You may know, up close and personal, the confusion that exists around you. As you read Habakkuk, think of how these words apply to your life.

Chapter 2 begins with Habakkuk responding positively with action. Can you imagine his instant reaction to the Babylonian threat to his city? He obviously saw the outer fortress had breaches in it; when he saw a need, he filled it. Probably gathering other "minutemen," he took turns guarding the wall ("I will stand. . . ." v. 1). Can you picture him marching on the ramparts, or crouching in its weakest place, watching carefully for the enemy in the distance and then standing boldly, chin up, prepared to give his life for the homeland? Weapon in hand, he probably mumbled in the silence, "They won't push through on my watch!" Who do you believe "he" is (v. 1)? At first glance, "he" could be God, but then it appears that Habakkuk ("I") gives an answer to the complaint, and so far he is the one complaining. Look again. Could it be that God ("I" used three times in v. 1), who has already *stationed Himself on the wall*, sees Habakkuk climbing up, and will look for what *Habakkuk* ("he") says, ready to give an answer to the prophet's complaints?

Verse 2 gives us the answer: it makes it clear that "I" in v. 1 is Habakkuk, as it presents God's clear response. Habakkuk ("I," used three times in v. 1), anticipates the voice of God, who will respond. Then, in turn, Habakkuk will answer the complaints *of God's people* as God has directed. He may feel the weight of his serious responsibility as the mediator between God and his neighbors. Imagine Habakkuk's surprise when God responds with something else he can do besides standing, waiting for the enemy's attack: Habakkuk can write God's words and share them with others. A runner might publish Habakkuk's words all around the nation! As you read verses 2–3, you can see clearly this is the voice of God, who wants his word plainly conveyed to His people. He promises His revelation at the appointed time. Verse 3 seems to speak to everyone's heart. It is a verse on which we can rely to encourage us. God is powerful, and though he lingers — at least, on our timetables — He will surely reveal himself *on time*, in His own timing. Verses 4–17 show God's condemnation toward the enemy outside their gates, but also toward His own people inside. As you read, highlight the words of encouragement hidden among the reprimands.

MAJORING ON THE MINOR PROPHET

1. When you think of common life today, do you feel your community is experiencing religious and moral bewilderment? Why or why not? In which ways? Who seems bewildered?

2. Habakkuk did something immediately, standing in the gap in the wall. What could you do immediately to "stand in the gap" for someone who is unprotected?

3. God told Habakkuk to write and to make it plain. As you receive revelation from God, what could you write to make it plain to others that God loves them, even in sinful times when they must face Him with honestly?

Write something in your journal as a legacy for your children, your community, or your church.

4. Read Habakkuk 2:3 and spend time celebrating our Lord, who is always on time, all the time.

5. Set aside time in a morning hour to meditate on God's revelation in Isaiah 21:8*b*, 11*b*–12; Psalm 130:5; and Psalm 5:3.

U SE YOUR IMAGINATION

1. Write a first-person paragraph or poem about how you feel as a woman who sees Habakkuk on the ramparts and hears what he says about God's punishment.

2. How can you share the following verses that will give hope and comfort in times of anxiety and crisis? (In a note? On a bulletin board? In a newspaper letter to the editor? In a handout to your Sunday School class? Under a refrigerator magnet? At the top of your bathroom mirror? In your journal? Other ideas?)

a)   "The righteous person will live by his faithfulness" (2:4*b*);

b)   "For the earth will be filled with the knowledge of the glory of the Lord as the waters cover the sea" (2:14);

c)   "The Lord is in his holy temple; let all the earth be silent before him" (2:20).

*F*OR FURTHER STUDY

Compare Habakkuk 2:11 with Luke 19:40, and Psalm 147, 148:1–13; 149; 150.

How do these passages assure you of God's sovereignty over all nature? Praise Him for His creation.

PRAISE THE LORD!

The final chapter of Habakkuk records his prayer of praise to God. As a musician, he probably raises his voice with praise as he plays his instruments. Imagine a string quartet of primitive instruments near the wall, playing as Habakkuk conducts, even in his time of fear and stress. He stands on the ramparts in awe of God, looking out over the valley (v. 1) and calls for God to renew His awesome deeds. Read reverently Habakkuk 3:1–2, recognizing God's deeds, then His glory (vv. 3–4,),and His power to deliver (vv. 5–15). Though Habakkuk is fearful (v. 16), he remains faithful and waits (vv. 17–18). His words crescendo in the last verse (v. 19) as he feels God's power enabling him to jump like a deer going to "the heights."

*M*AJORING ON THE MINORS

1. Thank God for past answered prayer, even when you couldn't see ahead that God was coming to your rescue. Tell a friend about verses 17–19, sharing how God is our strength, even when we see no fruit for our labor.

2. Habakkuk says, "Yet I will rejoice in the Lord, I will be joyful in God my Savior" (3:18), as he awaits the punishment of God. Most of us find that kind of submission and obedience hard to accomplish. What advice would you give another person who is having difficulty submitting to God's will?

3. How would you describe a deer's feet (3:19)? Which characteristics of a deer would be desirable for a worshiper? Which verses in this study have carried you to "the heights," as Habakkuk says? In your journal,

list other verses in the Bible which take you to the heights of spiritual inspiration.

4. Write in your journal your favorite ideas from this chapter. Memorize at least one verse.

U SE YOUR IMAGINATION

1. If you were a woman in Habakkuk's day, could you accept God's punishment and still praise Him, as Habakkuk did? Do you think Habakkuk was a fiery prophet or a gentle one? Why? What can we do to have his attitude?

2. What desire has God given you in response to the words of Habakkuk? How has God touched your spirit with His Spirit?

3. If you can, compose a song to perform for your family or Bible study group. You may, as Habakkuk probably did, compose a tune to go with your lyrics, or you can use a familiar tune you already know. It may be a dirge for the nation, a prayer/plea for forgiveness, or a praise chorus.

4. How do you believe you can you prepare for the future as you wait?

5. Write in your journal a revelation God may give to a modern-day Habakkuk. Depend on Habakkuk 2:2–3 for inspiration.

*F*OR FURTHER STUDY

In an attitude of praise, read Psalm 48:1. Ask your church worship leader/ music director to play "Great Is the Lord and Worthy of Praise." Ask a soloist to sing it at your Bible study gathering. Then read Psalm 48:3, 13–14, and Psalm 130:5–8.

> *Prayer: We stand in awe at Your deeds, Lord. Give us courage to serve faithfully in the gap where we're needed, to face the evil enemy. Give us the humility to confess our sins and the*

patience to wait on You. Thank You for rescuing us in Your timing, in Jesus' name, Amen.

JOURNAL FOR THE MAJORS IN MY LIFE

CHAPTER 9

Zephaniah: Town Crier to Jerusalem

by Edna Ellison

Be silent before the Sovereign Lord, for the day of the Lord is near. ZEPHANIAH 1:7

As a young housewife, God was deepening my Christian maturity, drawing me closer to Him. When our church hosted a revival that fall, I couldn't wait to pray during the around-the-clock vigil beforehand. My aunt kept my child that afternoon while I went to the church sanctuary to pray. At 2:30 I began, fervently asking God to bless our revival — that many unsaved people would come to know Him as Savior, and that efforts to draw people to the services would be successful. I prayed for our pastor and the visiting evangelist. I called the name of every nonbeliever I knew, praying for salvation. I prayed that God's Spirit would permeate our town and our entire region.

Whew! I was exhausted. I wondered if my hour was up. I looked at my watch: 2:35. I had prayed only five minutes! How could that be? I was discouraged, with nothing else to pray for. I fell silent, very uncomfortable.

All of a sudden, I heard a loud pop! Startled, I jumped in my seat. I looked around, but saw nothing out of the ordinary. *Maybe the cathedral ceiling had popped when the sun heated the roof.* The sanctuary continued to crack and

BACKGROUND

Zephaniah probably lived around 630 B.C., when this book was written. The name Zephaniah probably means "The Lord hides (protects)." Far from being a quiet man, he became the prophet to the people, a Town Crier in Jerusalem. With high social standing, a fourth-generation descendant of King Hezekiah, Zephaniah was familiar with royal court proceedings and knowledgeable about Jerusalem's political issues.

After Hezekiah died, Judah fell into moral decay. The next kings, Amon and Manasseh, allowed shameful practices of foreign cults in Jerusalem. Due to Scythian migration in the late seventh century B.C., ornate, imported clothes became popular even among the usually-modest Jews. Then when Josiah became king, he launched reform. Although contemporaries Jeremiah and Nahum joined Josiah in urging Judah's people to turn to God, the land remained corrupt. Zephaniah felt God's call to present a warning about judgment, a plea for repentance, and a reminder of His mercy.

pop, and then I heard someone open the door. *Thank goodness! Someone is here!* I closed my eyes, bowing my head to be in an attitude of prayer as the person entered. Then I peeked at the foyer. Since nobody was there, I returned to prayer.

After another boring half-hour, I realized I didn't know how to pray. God humbled me as I learned how to connect with His Spirit. That day before our church revival, I began my own heart revival, deepening my personal relationship with Him.

Humans are often afraid of silence. We rush from one thing to another, filling our lives with busyness so we don't have to be alone with God. We fill the air with music or TV/radio chatter, drowning out the Holy Spirit's whisper. Zephaniah's message is a cry to "be silent before the Lord."

THE BUSY CONSUMER (ZEPHANIAH 1:1–13)

Zephaniah lived in a noisy place. Read Zephaniah 1:1–13; make notes of sounds he might have heard in Jerusalem. He probably had to raise his voice to deliver God's message. Three areas are mentioned in these verses: (1) the market district, (2) religious places — like our churches, temples, or synagogues, and (3) residential subdivisions. Survey these verses, finding his warnings about the Day of the Lord, a major theme throughout this book. No doubt God's people had forgotten His goodness, becoming so busy with everyday life — maintaining the country's infrastructure, practicing religious liturgy, and keeping their family life intact — that they had neglected the original focus of their country, worshipping God.

Think of the average person in Zephaniah's day — a Jerusalem resident and busy consumer, buying food in the market, building bigger houses to store possessions, and purchasing jewelry to make a good impression in this fashionable city, the seat of government and commerce.

$\mathcal{M}$AJORING ON THE MINOR PROPHET

Can you identify with people in the three major areas of life in Zephaniah's day?

Since he perhaps was King Josiah's remote relative, what influence could he have had in the palace, the market district, and his residential neighborhood?

1. In your own words, describe the devastation Zephaniah predicts.

2. How do you think the merchants in the market district reacted?

3. What's your opinion of street evangelists, today's town criers, predicting the end of the world or the wrath of God?

Since Jesus was a marketplace evangelist, healing and speaking in public streets and other places, how do you think He would be treated today?

4. How would Animal Rights activists in today's world react to verses 2–3?

5. What do you think "remnant of Baal" means in verse 4?

What/who are our Baals today?

6. How do verses 7–9*a* and 12 describe complacency about worship?

7. If you made a poster with the same accusations God makes against the Jews in Jerusalem, what would you write?

* For more information on marketplace ministries, go to actionevangelism. org, associatedcontent.com, agm-ffci.org, and onmission.com.

U SE YOUR IMAGINATION

Play the game "I Spy" with a few Bible study friends. Take turns describing one character in today's study (maybe the wife of a courtly "royal" in Josiah's palace, a poor Jewish woman on the outskirts of Jerusalem, or a temple prostitute wearing sexy clothes from Moab.) For instance, "I spy another person like me wearing sackcloth and mourning in the temple. Joel should come where I work instead of preaching in the streets." [a priest, Joel 1:13] Whoever guesses the portrayed character says "I Spy. . . ." next.

1. Imagine you are Zephaniah, and God has given you these words to influence your city, state, or nation. Which avenues would you use to spread the message?

2. Unlike the figurative language used by other prophets like Joel, Zephaniah describes war in horrible, realistic terms. Imagine you're a wife inside a large secure home in Jerusalem. In your journal, write a short story (at least a paragraph or two) describing how your life changes as this prophecy unfolds.

THE DAY OF JUDGMENT

Dies irae, dies illa, a Latin translation of "The Day of the Lord" (literally, "day of wrath [ire], that day"), is an ancient Gregorian chant. Recorded in the liturgical calendar year as "The Hymn of the Church, in Meditation of the Day of Judgment," it ends with "Lord, have mercy, Jesus blest, grant them all Your Light and Rest. Amen." For a free mp3 download, search beemp3.com.

3. Compare your life to that of people in Zephaniah's Judah:

How do you receive messages of prophecy today?

What images of war are available?

Which people do you know who claim allegiance to God but swear by other "idols" (v. 5)?

How many do you know who "worship the starry host," perhaps in the astrology column of their newspaper?

How can you approach them with information about false beliefs?

4. Exactly how can you obey verse 7: "Be silent before the Sovereign Lord"?

Relinquishing busyness to sit in silence is hard. How would you advise someone to do it?

5. If you know people who've served in the military, ask them to share about battle experience, if they're willing. Make a prayer list. Ask others to join you in prayer for the military from your community.

THE DAY OF THE LORD (ZEPHANIAH 1:14 – 2:15)

The main theme of these verses is Zephaniah's phrase, "The Day of the Lord." God warned Judah, but also surrounding nations whom Judah had influenced, about the day of reckoning. We might assume that, like New York or Hong Kong today, some of the broader world's people might come to Jerusalem to shop, party, or invest in property. Visitors probably infiltrated commercial and religious institutions with pagan customs. Other nations would suffer along with Jerusalem because of their sinful involvement. They, like us, are responsible for their actions. Every action has consequences.

God's actions reflect His character: God is pure, too holy to live with sin. God is honest. He tells us — in writing, where all can read it — about punishment for sin. God is just. He must punish sin because He is holy, honest, and just.

$\mathcal{M}$AJORING ON THE MINOR PROPHET

1. List Zephaniah's words predicting the horrors of the Day of the Lord.

Based on 1:18, do you believe God has the right to be jealous of your love for Him?

2. What hope does Zephaniah 2:2–3 offer you?

3. Who, in verses 4–15, were those who would receive God's punishment?

4. If you were God's prosecuting attorney in this court district, what evidence shows they deserve conviction for crimes?

U SE YOUR IMAGINATION

Imagine you're a woman in the courtyard of the Jerusalem temple and you hear Zephaniah shouting, "Seek the Lord, all you humble of the land, you who do what he commands. Seek righteousness, seek humility; perhaps you will be sheltered on the day of the Lord's anger" (2:3). How would she react? You might hope her heart would be broken over the city's sin. She might have bowed her head, begging God to save her and to renew His Spirit within her. Today would we react as righteously as a humble believer then? As Christians we desire to seek the Lord, doing what He commands. We know God speaks His words to us as He did to people in Jerusalem. How would you react in the following scenarios?

1. Imagine you're one of the women living in a nation near Judah.

    How would you describe your heart's cry over the situation in verses 4–15?

    How might you protect your family against this crisis?

    Given the status of women in the Old Testament, what choices could you make?

2. As a Jewish doctor, nurse, or advocate for children, what actions would you take?

3. If you were a judge, senator, or temple staff, how could you respond?

    Given the status of women today, what choices could you make?

4. Today many of us seek a carefree life of safety and comfort. Using Zephaniah 2:13–15, how can you help your friends — or yourself — avoid following Nineveh's city motto: "I am, and there is none besides me"?

REJOICE IN THE LORD (ZEPHANIAH 3)

In Zephaniah 3 God addresses women personally: "Sing, O Daughter of Zion; shout aloud, O Israel! Be glad and rejoice with all your heart" (3:14). Just before this passage, Zephaniah condemns them, warning of war and punishment. He describes sins (Zephaniah 3:1–5), and then vows to assemble nations for punishment, restoring dignity to the righteous remnant: meek, humble, and unafraid (vv. 6–13). Immediately, he begins a glorious passage (vv. 15–20) comforting them and outlining five things He will do (v. 17):

- "The Lord your God is with you." Engaged couples spend time together, demonstrating their love by being near as much as possible. God, who loves you more than any human lover, is always with you, as close as a heartbeat. Vigilantly watching over you, He "will neither slumber nor sleep". . . [but watches] "over your coming and going both now and forevermore" (Psalm 121:4, 8).

- "He is mighty to save." Despite decades of wickedness, God promised to save a remnant of His people (v. 12). Sometimes we forget He has all power, money, heavenly blessings, and comfort. Most of all, He provides eternal life through His Son's sacrifice.

  God also promises — in writing — angels will watch over us: "Are not all angels ministering spirits sent to serve those who will inherit salvation" (Hebrews 1:14)? "For he will command his angels . . . to guard you in all your ways" (Psalm 91:11).

§ "He will take great delight in you." Do your parents or children grin when they're with you? How about a dog jumping up and down, wagging its tail? God cherishes your smile, your words — everything about you, with far more love than anyone.

§ "He will quiet you with his love." Jerusalem citizens were too busy to take time to stand humbly, silently before God. They were making money, buying new camels, consuming delicious food and wine. They just never got around to living out their intentions to love God.

We may regret we don't have time to worship Him, but we don't know what to do about the situation. We must impress our supervisor at work, be superwoman in the community, and provide catering and taxi services for our families. Some take care of babies or sick parents, caught in the sandwich generation. Yet in our frantic activity, we desire a personal relationship with the Master. We yearn to let Him quiet us with His overflowing love.

§ "He will rejoice over you with singing." I love the songs we sing at church: "Jesus is the Sweetest Name I Know" or "Majesty! Worship His Majesty." We love to praise Jesus, rejoicing over *Him*, but this verse surprises us: *He* rejoices over *us*! Imagine how much He loves you. Barbara Ann Moore, my friend who read these words, asked, "If God is rejoicing over me, could he be singing 'Bar-bar-bar-Barbara Ann, Bar-bar-bar-Barbara Ann . . . ?'" I trust, because He loves you, He's singing your song today!

As you sit quietly before God, allow Him to show (1) He is with you, (2) He is mighty to save you, (3) He will take great delight in you, (4) He will quiet you with His love, and (5) He will rejoice over you with singing.

MAJORING ON THE MINOR PROPHET

1. Remember when you fell in love with your spouse and you never wanted
    to leave his side? Write those memories in your journal.

    How can you compare God's love to earthly love?

    What does it mean to lean on God's *everlasting* arms?

2. Compare Psalm 91:9–16 to Zephaniah 3:17. In your journal, record
    ideas about these promises.

3. Write your favorite promises in Zephaniah that have a positive influ-
    ence on your life.

*U*SE YOUR IMAGINATION

Fast forward to the time following the destruction of Jerusalem in 587/86 B.C., after Nebuchadnezzar had conquered the city in 597. Zephaniah's prediction had come true. Thousands have been killed. The Jewish establishment has been scattered, taken as slaves to Babylon. The loyal remnant has been saved, and secretly they are worshiping the one true God.

1. Imagine you're a poor Jerusalem woman who's experienced foreign troops sweeping through your city, finding yourself left behind. How can you begin to rebuild your life?

   What kinds of devotion can you give God?

2. Spend time with God today — regardless of what you must sacrifice to do it. Zephaniah urges us to give God uppermost priority in our lives. How can we find ways to simplify?

   How can you make time for quiet moments with God?

3. Plan a God spa in a quiet place, a day of fasting and prayer. (Fruit juice and water are acceptable.) Arrange your calendar to fellowship with God for an extended period. Use your Bible, a journal, and other worship aids. If you have fears of the future, lay them before God. If He calls to mind sins in your life, confess them. Write in your journal what you feel God is saying.

4. As a result, what are you inspired to change in your lifestyle? Write these options in your journal to set goals later.

5. From personal experience, do you know what it means to be "saved," or "born again"? If not, read God's Plan of Salvation at the back of this book.

*F*OR FURTHER STUDY

For more information on this era, read Jeremiah; Nahum; 2 Kings 21:24 to 23:34; "That Day of Wrath, That Dreadful Day," *Nelson's Compact Illustrated Bible Dictionary*, pp. 283, Nashville: Thomas Nelson Publishers, 1964; and http://en.wikipedia.org.

Prayer: Almighty God, help us not to fear, whatever our circumstances. Thank You for giving us total trust in You, peace during every life-storm, and hope for the future. Give us courage to face any crisis with serenity, and equip us to serve You one day at a time. Amen.

$\mathcal{J}$OURNAL FOR THE MAJORS IN MY LIFE

CHAPTER 10

Haggai: Rebuilder of Hope

by Tricia Scribner

'The glory of this present house will be greater than the glory of the former house,' says the LORD Almighty. 'And in this place I will grant peace,' declares the LORD Almighty." HAGGAI 2:9

Imagine you dreamed of building a village to house and protect hungry and abandoned children in a drought-stricken Third-World country. It was a good dream, motivated by benevolent concern. You travelled to the country, and you hired an architect to design the small homes in which the children would live with house parents you had already interviewed and hired. You enlisted sponsors to pay for their schooling and clothes, located the most needy children, and brought them to the site with great hopes of their starting new lives filled with new hopes and dreams. But you forgot one critical piece of the puzzle. You forgot to obtain food and water sources. The faucets were dry as a bone and the pantries were filled only with empty shelves.

Not knowing what is most important can yield catastrophic results. The Israelites returning from their 70-year exile in Babylon learned this truth the hard way. Both the northern kingdom of Israel, consisting of ten tribes, and the southern kingdom of Judah, with two tribes, had skirmished with their occupying overlords. For northern Israel the end came with the invasion

ARCHAEOLOGY SUPPORTS THE BIBLICAL ACCOUNT

Is it really possible that a foreign king allowed the Jewish people to return to their homeland and rebuild their temple of worship? Extrabiblical archaeological evidence corroborates the biblical record. The Cyrus Cylinder, a baked clay cylinder 23 cm long and 11 cm wide, was discovered in 1879. In about 40 lines of writing, the cylinder records Cyrus's peaceful takeover of Babylon and his view that conquered peoples be allowed to return to their homelands and even rebuild their temples of worship. The cylinder is now housed in the British Museum in London. The biblical account also accords with first-century Jewish historian Josephus's assertion that King Cyrus became aware of Isaiah's prophecy (written about 200 years before Cyrus lived) that a king named Cyrus would grant permission for the Jews to return to their homeland and that he desired to personally fulfill the prophecy.

by the ruling empire Assyria's Shalmaneser V in 722/21 B.C., by which the Northern Kingdom was decimated and its people hauled into exile (2 Kings 17:1–6).

The prophets continued to warn Israel's southern sister, Judah, but the prophets' messages fell on deaf ears, and eventually Judah's people witnessed first-hand the worst imaginable tragedy of the entire Israelite nation, the destruction and setting fire to Jerusalem's walls and the temple. With the stench of her burning monument to God's presence still in her nostrils, a new reigning power, Babylon, dragged away Judah's citizens in several exportations from 605 to 587/86 B.C. The Scriptures record that only the poorest citizens, ones too weak to foment another rebellion, were left in the land to care for the remaining crops and vines.

Eventually, about 539 B.C., the Medo-Persian Empire took over the Near East with Cyrus the Great at the helm. Desiring to build goodwill and allegiance even among the conquered people within his kingdom, and with admirable political acumen — if history's treatment of him is any indication — Cyrus issued a landmark decree in 538 B.C. that the Jews could return to their homeland and rebuild their temple. The exiles returned in three waves over about 100 years (Zerubbabel led the first return in 537/36 B.C. of about 50,000, according to Ezra 2:4 [see also Ezra 2:1–2]; Ezra led the second group in 458/57 B.C.; and Nehemiah led the third group as governor in 444 B.C.).

The first returnees entered their homeland to find that the heartbeat of their nation, the temple, lay in a heap of crumbled debris. The land was suffering a throat-parching drought, and the weeds had consumed the formerly lush cropland. Into such bleak circumstances walked the prophet Haggai to announce God's message of exhortation to His people. It was the kind of situation God is famous for using to His glory and His people's blessing.

REFLECT AS YOU REBUILD (HAGGAI 1:1–15)

By the time Haggai came on the scene, Persia had amassed control of a huge area under Cyrus's favorable 30-year rule (559–530 B.C.). Their land holdings stretched from northern Africa to the southern part of Russia and from Asia Minor to India. Cyrus's rule was followed by that of his foolish son Cambyses (530–522 B.C.), who died while king. Darius I Hystaspes (not the Darius in Daniel's day) took power in 522 B.C. Haggai 1:1 tells us that in Darius's second year of reign — which would be 520 B.C. since the Persians did not count the first partial year — when a king arose to the throne, Haggai proclaimed his first message to God's people in their homeland. Though repairs had begun some 16 years prior, the temple itself still lay in ruins. Haggai spoke his first message on the first day of the month, the usual day of offerings and celebration, emphasizing both in its wording and also in its timing the misplaced priorities of God's people as an explanation for their current destitution in their own homeland.

Read 1:1–11. Haggai spoke directly to the representative leaders of God's people, Zerubbabel, the governor who had led the first of three returns back to Israel, and Joshua, the high priest, who had quite a challenge in leading the people to worship when the LORD's holy temple lay like a behemoth rotting elephant in the middle of the room. Why had they not completed the rebuilding? For one thing, they had been busy building their own "paneled houses" (NASB). Having lived so long like an unwelcomed distant cousin in a foreign land made them understandably eager to settle in back at home. But clearly their priorities were all wrong. While God's house lay fallow, they had abandoned kingdom priorities for temporal ones.

In all fairness, the job of rebuilding God's temple had not been an easy one. Ezra, who recorded much about the same time period, described their difficulties in Ezra 4:4–5. Evidently the local inhabitants weren't too excited about the Jews returning and rebuilding what the Jews themselves viewed as the seat of their God and the glory of their nation, and tried to thwart their efforts at every turn. Nevertheless, before we excuse them, we must remember that God has always enabled all He asks us to do, and their lack of rebuilding was not due to opposition but to lack of obedience and trust in the God who was more than able to accomplish the task if they had been willing and faithful.

In Haggai 1:5–11 the prophet urged them twice to consider or reflect on what they were doing in light of God's view. Isn't it good sometimes just to stop and think? Take a moment and recognize the mess for what it is: a mess! It was true that the Jews were home, but home surely was not what they remembered. The land that had once produced a bountiful harvest was unyielding, and the sky withheld its rain. And to add insult to injury, God announced that He was the author of these desolate circumstances. Why? Every parent of teens knows this principle. When you've got a strong-willed child, sometimes you have to let him experience the full weight of his actions' consequences before the recalcitrant child understands he even has a problem. So this is what God did. He let them dig the sun-baked soil until their knuckles were raw and plant enough seed to produce a barn-filling harvest only to find the seeds blew away in the blistering wind and those that sprouted just as quickly wilted in the heat.

Now that the people understood they had a problem and the reason for it, in verses 7–11 God, through Haggai, told His people what they needed to do to remedy the problem. Redirecting their efforts away from building themselves homes, they were to go bring wood to rebuild God's house with one goal in mind: to please and glorify the LORD. They were to abandon their self-consumed ways and consume themselves with their God.

Remember when I said that what God asks of us He always enables? Haggai closed his message in verses 12–15 with the assurance that the people would not complete this job through teeth-gritting human will. Rather, God would dwell within, energize, and accomplish His purpose through the exercise of their feet-moving faith. In God's mind the temple was a done deal, a completed task, because when God's people make what's important to God important to them, even hell's minions can't stop the project from getting done.

$\mathcal{M}$AJORING ON THE MINOR PROPHET

1. What was wrong with the people's attitudes about rebuilding God's temple?

2. Since they had legitimate obstacles, why did God view their justifications as excuses rather than acceptable reasons for not completing the temple rebuilding project?

3. Read Matthew 6:19–33.

a. How does this passage echo the message of Haggai 1:1–15?

b. What does God promise us when we make His kingdom priorities our own?

4. How did the promise of God's presence transform the people's view of the intimidating assignment?

U SE YOUR IMAGINATION

1. List areas the Lord has revealed to you during this study in which you need to rethink your priorities.

2. If what God viewed as important you also viewed with the same importance, which of your priorities would have to change? Specifically, how would they change?

3. Write a note to the Lord, confessing misplaced priorities and documenting actions you will take this week to put feet to your plan.

REMEMBER AS YOU REBUILD (HAGGAI 2:1–9)

When people try to impress me with their account of some amazing musical concert they've attended, I just smugly reply, "You think that was something. I saw Elvis in concert in 1975!" Usually they look at me, stunned. I'm not sure whether it's because I'm confessing how old I am or because to see Elvis live in concert is a memorable experience. Regardless, once you've seen Elvis, no other performer really compares. I imagine the Israelites felt similarly about Solomon's temple.

Read Haggai 2:1–9. In its former glory the temple was an amazing sight to behold, the dwelling of God's very presence, and the national point of pride. Likely, a few of the elderly returnees actually remembered how it looked before it was ransacked and burned by Nebuchadnezzar's forces some 70 years prior. In fact, Ezra 3:12 says that about 16 years before, when they had made the first effort to rebuild the temple's foundation, while there was great joy, many of the elderly who had seen the first temple actually wept. So now they had to fight the "Why bother?" mentality. There was no way their efforts could yield a temple with half the glory of the temple they remembered. So Haggai in his second message spoke to Zerubbabel, Joshua, and the people, helping them get their focus off the situation and put it where it needed to be.

Though the first temple was indeed glorious, and by comparison the current temple in its decrepit state must have looked pitiful, he reminded them of a transforming truth: the same God who led them safely out of Egypt into their homeland was with them now. He continued by laying out a future that reached even beyond their earthly lives. The temple's current state of disrepair was a mere shadow of what was to come, and they could be a part of the temple's magnificent future if they would pick up a shovel and just do their part. The final fulfillment of this promise is yet to come. When we look at the Muslim Dome of the Rock on the temple mount in Jerusalem, we can know that it is only temporary, for "the latter glory of this house will be greater than the former, says the LORD of hosts, and in this place I shall give peace, declares the LORD of hosts" (Haggai 2:9 NASB).

*M*AJORING ON THE MINOR PROPHET

1. On what did the people initially focus that caused discouragement?

2. List God's commands and promises in this passage that would transform their focus from earthly to kingdom priorities.

*U*SING YOUR IMAGINATION

1. What situation in your life seems so hopeless you have lost courage and have quit trying to rebuild?

2. How does this passage change your understanding of what your focus should be as you face the situation with courage?

REPENT AS YOU REBUILD (HAGGAI 2:10–19)

Imagine eating a meal off a dish from which someone else just finished eating. Not too appetizing. Read Haggai 2:10–19. Haggai used a similar example to make a spiritual point. God's people were as spiritually unclean due to lack of repentance as they would be ritually unclean from their clothes touching a dead body. They needed to understand that God could not be bought with "doing." God was pleased and He blessed them because they repented and changed in their "being." Thus, it was not the temple transformation but the people's heart transformation that brought them into right relationship with their God.

The glad result of repentance was restoration: of the relationship, of hope, and of the land itself. God assured them that hope was tangible and imminent. In verse 19, He set a date marker so people would know whom to credit for the return of the rains and the harvest. "But from this day [forward]" (NKJV) things would change!

MAJORING ON THE MINOR PROPHET

1. According to God, why had the land not been fruitful?

2. Haggai repeated the command to "consider" (NASB) in both 2:15 and 18, reminiscent of his instruction to "consider" in 1:5 and 7. What differences do you see between the implications of "consider" in the first and second chapters?

U SING YOUR IMAGINATION

1. In what areas of your life do you need to repent and restore your fellowship with God?

2. How have you tried to please God merely in your "doing" rather than in your "being"?

REJOICE AS YOU REBUILD (HAGGAI 2:20–23)

As you read this passage, consider the following. Before the exile of Judah's people the prophets had warned that if they continued to follow their sister Israel's evil ways, they would be exiled. Two of Judah's kings, Jehoiakin and his son Jehoichin, like many of the nation's kings, were described as wicked (see 2 Kings 24). Though in the messianic family line of David, they certainly did not live up to their family name and calling. In fact, Jeremiah (22:24–30) described God's rejection of them in grief-stricken terms. "Even if you, Jehoiachin son of Jehoiakim king of Judah, were a signet ring on my right hand, I would still pull you off."

What was a signet ring? Worn on a cord around the neck or as a ring for the hand, in ancient times the signet ring bore the unique engraving of the wearer. Documents could be sealed with a daub of clay imprinted with the ring's unique markings to authenticate its contents as those of the ring bearer.

Nevertheless, God is faithful and His plans will not be thwarted, and God guarantees His promises will come true. Zerubbabel was His seal, His signet, the sign that God remembered His people and assured their future.

*M*AJORING ON THE MINOR PROPHET

1. In verses 20–22 how did Haggai's description of what God was going to do among the nations actually assure Judah of His presence and protection?

2. What was God's purpose, do you think, in calling Zerubbabel His "signet ring"?

*U*SING YOUR IMAGINATION

1. What old patterns or family history tends to discourage you from trying to change?

2. How does knowing God has chosen you and you are precious to Him give you courage to change and rebuild?

Prayer: Lord God, You want to do some rebuilding in my life. You have shown me how to think rightly about the situation, remember You are with me, repent where needed, and rejoice that my future is secure in You. Now, I commit to move forward, trusting You. Amen.

JOURNAL FOR THE MAJORS IN MY LIFE:

CHAPTER 11

Zechariah: Restorer of Vision

by Tricia Scribner

*Therefore tell the people: This is what the Lord Almighty says:
"Return to me," declares the Lord Almighty, "and I will return
to you," says the Lord Almighty.* ZECHARIAH 1:3

Have you ever pondered a problem all day long, turning it over and over in your mind, only to find the solution came unbidden as you fell asleep? Some of my most valuable insights have come during those twilight moments before sleep. Zechariah could identify with my preslumber "aha" incidences. He is known for eight graphic visions about the future of his nation that the Lord gave him one after the other, all in one night.

Zechariah likely arrived in Jerusalem with his priestly family as part of the initial group of returnees under the direction of Zerubbabel about 520 B.C. Like Haggai, Zechariah was called to spur on the completion of the temple, a project that had been stalled for some 16 years by the time he began his ministry. You will remember that Haggai preached four messages in that same year, urging the people to complete the temple project. One month before Haggai finished his series of four messages, Zechariah picked up the theme, sort of tag-teaming with Haggai and continuing his messages for two more years into 518 B.C. Many scholars believe that Zechariah wrote the first eight chapters during this initial period of time from 520 and 518 B.C. and then later in his life wrote the prophetic chapters of 9–14.

RETURN TO ME AND I WILL RETURN
TO YOU IN AMAZING WAYS (1:1 TO 8:23)

In the first half of the book (chaps. 1–8) Zechariah the prophet spoke three messages. The first is recorded in 1:1–6. As you read these verses, note that Zechariah's first message urged the people not to mimic their ancestors' rebellion. Instead, Zechariah announced, God had called them to return to Him in repentance. On the condition of their turning, God would once again dwell among and bless His chosen people.

The second message, in 1:7 to 6:15, was comprised of eight visions Zechariah received while pondering the nation's problems one night. Zechariah's visions were filled with vivid imagery. If you find them difficult to understand, know that Zechariah himself asked for clarification numerous times regarding the meaning of the visions. Though details may be difficult to grasp, we can focus on the main truth embedded in each vision. Each one addressed a specific problem of the nation, giving hope and direction to God's people through His messenger, Zechariah. As we review the visions, concentrate

Who was the Angel of the LORD? In Zechariah's first vision (1:11) he identified this figure as the man who stood among the myrtle trees. Taking the comments of other Old Testament passages in which this figure is mentioned, it is reasonable to conclude that He is the pre-incarnate Son, known during His earthly life as Jesus Christ. Read Genesis 16:7-13 where He gave Hagar a promise only God could give, 22:11-12 where He saved Isaac's life as Abraham was ready to obey God and slay him, Exodus 3:2-6 where He appeared to Moses in the burning bush, and Judges 6:11-23 where He appeared to Gideon to strengthen him for victory in battle.

on the main point for each that God wished the people to understand and apply in their lives. Remember also that God's vision for the nation of Israel is still awaiting its ultimate fulfillment.

In the first vision of 1:8–17 Zechariah saw a man standing among myrtle trees. He had sent out four horsemen to patrol the earth who returned to Him announcing peace, at least temporarily, on the earth. The Angel of the LORD responded with a lament for the people of Jerusalem, to which God responded with tender, compassionate words of promise that the temple would indeed be rebuilt and His holy city would prosper.

Zechariah's second vision of 1:18–21 revealed four horns or government powers that had scattered the people of Judah. Workers called craftsmen appeared and overthrew the powers. The builders of the temple, the craftsmen, would be the "soldiers" God would use to defeat Israel's oppressors, not by armed warfare, but by completing the temple through which God would once again be declared as ruler of the nation and display His power and love for Israel.

Third, in 2:1–5 a man preparing to measure the expanse of Jerusalem was assured that one day the city would be filled to overflowing with people. Moreover, God Himself would form a wall of fire around the city and shine as her glory from within. Imagine the hope this promise instilled in God's people as they looked over the temple's rubble.

In the fourth vision, recorded in 3:1–10 Joshua, the priest who returned with Zerubbabel, was challenged by enemies but was confirmed by God Himself. In his vision Zechariah observed that Joshua's filthy garments were exchanged for pure white robes that heralded a day when the Branch, or Shoot, a descendant of Zerubbabel, would remove filthiness once and for all from the land. While Zechariah may have envisioned Zerubbabel fulfilling this role, we know from our vantage some 2,500 years later that the perfect fulfillment of this prophecy will occur when Messiah returns.

In Zechariah's fifth vision, described in 4:1–14, a seven-stemmed lampstand, or menorah, signifying the fullness of God's vision appeared with the two olive trees, Judah's leaders Zerubbabel and Joshua, standing alongside. Through this vision God assured that the nation's leaders, chosen by God, would accomplish God's plan to rebuild, not by a sheer act of will, but by God's empowerment.

A flying scroll measuring about 30 by 15 feet showed up in Zechariah's sixth vision of 5:1–4. On the scroll was inscribed God's curse upon the wicked people of Judah who stole and bore false witness. The returnees needed to understand that God had not changed in the interim while they were exiled. The same evil that had landed their ancestors in exile would still warrant God's judgment.

In his seventh vision of 5:5–11 Zechariah saw a basket in which sat a woman who represented wickedness in 5:5–11. The basket with the woman inside was then air lifted to Shinar, or Babylon, and placed in a temple designed for her. Clearly, God still hated false pagan religions and would purge them from the land.

Finally, the eighth vision recorded in 6:1–8, revealed chariots and riders entering the north land, a reference to Babylon, eventually reporting to Zechariah that God's Spirit had settled there. While scholars suggest several interpretations, it seems that Babylon would be judged, bringing the dominion and peace of God's Spirit to rest there. God then told Zechariah in 6:9–15 to take an offering from God's people who remained in Babylon and crown Joshua to symbolize God's crowning of the Branch, or Messiah, Who would one day come as universal Ruler.

After the second message's eight visions and meanings were shared with Zechariah, and then with the people, the prophet in 7:1–14 proclaimed a third message. More than ritual fasting, God wanted the people to obey Him. God reminded them that the very cause of their exile had been their unwillingness to do what God had asked and instead going their own way. Unless the external rituals expressed the genuine worship of a pure heart, they had accomplished nothing. The third message closed out with chapter 8, in which the prophet was given the key to his entire prophetic ministry regarding the coming millennial reign of Messiah. Read the description of the future concerning God's land and His people in 8:3–5, 7–8, and 20–23. Clearly, this prophecy anticipates a future fulfillment. Imagine the land of Israel one day being the darling instead of the reproach of the nations!

*M*AJORING ON THE MINOR PROPHET

1. Read Zechariah 1:8–9 and 4:1–5. What evidence do you see that Zechariah, like us, had difficulty understanding the meaning of his visions?

2. List each of the eight visions and briefly explain what significance each held for Judah's future. In other words, if the people believed God's message revealed in each vision, how would they need to respond? I have completed the first one for you as an example.

    1. Man among the myrtle trees: God would complete the temple if they would be obedient, and He would guarantee a wonderful future if only they would love and obey Him.

    2.

    3.

4.

5.

6.

7.

8.

$\mathcal{U}$ SE YOUR IMAGINATION

1. After reading Zechariah 4:6, think about a situation in which you need to remember that God's purposes will be accomplished not by might nor power but by God's Spirit. Write below a prayer of trust in the Lord.

2. Read Zechariah 4:10. God accomplishes big things through the faithful completion of small things. God's promise of a glorious future for Israel would be (and shall be) accomplished. What small things have you avoided doing, perhaps because of discouragement, that God would have you now tackle in faith so that His plan can be fulfilled for and through you?

THE KING WILL COME AND FACE REJECTION
(ZECHARIAH 9:1 TO 11:17)

As we discussed, the second half of the book was likely written long after the temple-oriented messages of the first eight chapters. In fact, after chapter 8, the temple is never again mentioned. Further, there are no more date references, and no more references to Zechariah, Zerubbabel or Joshua. Another indication of a later date is that the prophet no longer mentioned the Persians, instead preaching about Greece, the power that arose after the decline of Persia.

This half of the book can be divided into two oracles or messages presented by Zechariah, the first recorded in chapters 9–11, and the final message recorded in chapters 12–14.

In Zechariah 9 the writer announced judgment for oppressing nations and then introduced Messiah as King, coming to Zion. The prophecy in 9:9 described Messiah's future triumphal entry into Jerusalem, an entry like no other earthly king's: humbly, on a donkey's colt.

UNITY WITHIN THE "TWELVE"

The books of the twelve minor prophets were viewed among the Jews as a single book and simply called "The Twelve" or "The Twelve Prophets." As you've studied them, you may have noticed repeating themes. For example, read Zechariah 13:9, noting the end time promise that a third of God's people would survive and be refined like silver and tested like gold. Zechariah then said God would claim them as His people and they would claim Him as their God. Now, flip back to the first book of the Twelve in the Jewish Bible, Hosea, (just as in the English Bible) and read 2:23. Hosea described the people as ones about whom God would say, "You are my people, and they will say, 'You are my God.'" Now, turn to the end of the Twelve and read Malachi 3:3. You'll see the description of God as a "refiner's fire" Who will "purify . . . and refine them like gold and silver." Zechariah's quote, then, demonstrates one of many

The description of God's blessing on His people continued into chapter 10. Read 10:6–10. The LORD promised that the house of Judah, the Southern Kingdom, and the house of Joseph, the Northern Kingdom, would one day reunite in the land. Now, remember that Zechariah wrote this section later in life after the temple had been rebuilt and spoke of a time in the future when the people would be fully restored to the land. While some former citizens of the Northern Kingdom joined the Southern Kingdom returnees in repopulating Judah during Zechariah's lifetime, these returns were miniscule in comparison to the promised return in the future of God's people to their homeland.

In chapter 11 the prophet described a time of sorrow before the final restoration due to God's people rejecting the Good Shepherd in favor of a worthless shepherd. Despite the Shepherd's tender care of His people, they valued the Shepherd's work among them at a mere 30 shekels of silver, the

unifying themes occurring across the Twelve and Zechariah's prophecy and its wording connect the beginning (Hosea) to the end (Malachi).

pitiful compensation price for the accidental death of a slave (Exodus 21:32).

$\mathcal{M}$AJORING ON THE MINOR PROPHET

1. Read Zechariah 9:9; John 12:14–15 and Matthew 21:1–5. Write in the margins of your Bible the cross references for each verse beside the other verses. How does this prophecy's fulfillment support the trustworthiness of the Bible? Notice that the prophecy stated that Messiah would ride not only on a donkey, but on a donkey's colt. Jesus knew exactly where the donkey and colt would be found and also that the owner would allow the animals to be taken by the disciples.

2. Read Zechariah 11:12–13; Matthew 26:14–16 and 27:1–5. List similarities between the Old and New Testament descriptions of the people's treatment of their Shepherd.

*U*SE YOUR IMAGINATION

1. Read Jeremiah 29:11.When was the last time you wondered whether the Good Shepherd had your best interest at heart or questioned His goodness? Write the Lord a note expressing your grief at not trusting Him and expressing your trust in His good intentions toward you.

2. Imagine what your life would be like right now without the Good Shepherd providing His purpose, protection, and hope in every situation. How would your life be different without the knowledge that God held you closely to His heart?

THE KING WILL RETURN VICTORIOUS
(ZECHARIAH 12:1 TO 14:21)

While faithlessness, oppression, and rejection of Messiah have plagued the Israelite nation throughout history, the cycle will one day end. Before things get better they will get much worse though. There will be a time marked by an all-out assault on Jerusalem by foreign nations, but they will not have the ultimate victory.

The LORD Himself will intercede, planting His feet on the Mount of Olives, splitting it in two and opening a way of escape for the Jewish people (14:4–5). This time will be characterized by a return of the Jewish people to faith in Messiah (12:10–12) and the end of idolatry (13:1–5). Even the remnants of the foreign nations will worship the Lord (14:16–21).

*M*AJORING ON THE MINOR PROPHET

1. Read Zechariah 12:3, 8; 13:1, 4; 14:6, looking for two words repeated in each verse. Which day is "that day" to which these verses refer? Read 14:1 to find out. The Day of the LORD refers to the future ultimate time of judgment.

2. Read Amos 1:1, noting the mention of an earthquake occurring. During earthquakes people seek to flee the terror of the ground shaking. Now read Zechariah 14:3–5. How will the people respond similarly in the final cataclysmic battle over the city of Jerusalem when the Lord returns, stands on the Mount of Olives, and it splits in two?

3. Now read 1 Thessalonians 4:13–18. Notice that in the First Thessalonians passage the Lord comes in the air and the saints (believers) go to be with Him, whereas in the Zechariah prophecy (14:3–5) He plants His feet on the Mount of Olives and the saints return with Him. These descriptions give us insight into the two phases of Christ's Second Coming according to the pre-tribulation view of the end times, the first phase being known as the Rapture and the second the Glorious Return.

4. Read Zechariah 13:7; Matthew 26:31–35 and 47–56. How was Zechariah's prophecy specifically fulfilled during Jesus' arrest?

$\mathcal{U}$ SE YOUR IMAGINATION

1. Read Zechariah 12:10–12. Write a prayer for the Jewish people that God hasten their return to Messiah. Ask for the Lord's strength and boldness for missionaries who are now ministering among the Jewish people.

2. The last half of Zechariah focuses on Christ's millennial reign. Read Zechariah 14:16–21. List some of the changes to occur during the millennial reign recorded here by Zechariah. How do you think these changes would impact your life during the millennium?

Prayer: Lord Jesus, Your vision for the Jewish people, the nations of the world, and even for me is true in every way and trustworthy. Please show me how I may fulfill Your vision for my life and join You in establishing Your eternal kingdom on earth. Amen.

JOURNAL FOR THE MAJORS IN MY LIFE:

CHAPTER 12

Malachi: Covenant Contender

by Kimberly Sowell

"On the day when I act," says the LORD *Almighty, "they will be my treasured possession. I will spare them, just as a father has compassion and spares his son who serves him."* MALACHI 3:17

As I read a book about the Ten Commandments to my children, I got three distinct reactions from my three unique children. My four-year-old accepted each commandment as "you're not supposed to be bad" rules, and he felt sure he wasn't *too* guilty on any count. My five-year-old son, who had recently experienced a major dose of corrective discipline, openly admitted his guilt and his desire to mend his ways. My eight-year-old Christian daughter was the most intriguing participant in this review of the Ten Commandments. She is rarely in trouble at home and never in trouble at school, so she easily earns "good kid" status. However, as we read through God's laws, she often looked at me with an "oops" expression, or she buried her face in a pillow with embarrassment. She was guilty, and she knew that I knew it as much as she did, because of conversations she and I had finished just moments earlier!

Sin is ugly no matter who the sinner is, but sin from God's people is especially unbecoming because we are God's children. In the Book of Malachi, we read an ugly back-and-forth interchange between a loving God presenting His case of judgment and love to His people, and His people arguing with Him at every point. We see the patience of God and the smallness and arrogance of mankind. How could the children of Israel dare to challenge God? Despite their contentious bickering with God, He was merciful to them, because it is His good nature: "'I the LORD do not change. So you, the descendants of Jacob, are not destroyed'" (Malachi 3:6). God's patience shines forth in this book that culminates in the promise of redemption.

HE LOVES ME, HE LOVES ME NOT (MALACHI 1)

God had several charges to bring against His people; where should He begin? He began at the beginning—a most serious charge, and terribly personal between God and His people — they had doubted His love. It's not uncommon for young children to out with "you don't love me!" to a parent when he or she is suffering discipline, and the children of Israel had also been feeling the consequences of their actions. However, God had given them plenty of reason to know of His love for them, even during times of chastening.

The strongest piece of evidence was God's very words: "'I have loved you'" (1:2). God also reminded them they are His chosen people as the sons of Jacob. God chose Jacob the younger twin, instead of Esau the older twin, to be the recipient of their father Isaac's blessing and birthright, and God's promise (Genesis 28:10–15). The prideful Edomites (Esau's descendants) would be brought low, but the Israelites would see God's glory going forth beyond their borders.

FAST FACT
God demanded that cattle, sheep, and goats brought for sacrifice must be without blemish or defect, must not be sick, lame, or blind, and should not have warts or an infected wound (Leviticus 22:17-22).

Despite God's love for the children of Israel, they were not reciprocating that love. The priests dishonored and disrespected God by cheapening the sacrificial system with unsatisfactory animals. The people wouldn't dare try to get away with such robbery with their governor (Malachi 1:8), a human authority, but they didn't fear God any more than to try to cheat the great King (1:14).

MAJORING ON THE MINOR PROPHET

1. Rather than asking the question, "Why would God hate Esau?" (Malachi 1:3), ask the question, "Why would God love Jacob?" (1:2). Does any man or woman deserve God's love and forgiveness?

2. Read Hebrews 10:11–14. Since the animal sacrifice system led up to Jesus as the final and perfect Sacrifice, why was it important that the animals offered for sacrifice be "without blemish" (Exodus 12:5 NKJV)?

3. The children of Israel were offering less than their best to God for animal sacrifices, but they weren't sparing with the government authorities (Malachi 1:8). Why would they fear God less than the government authorities? In modern times, how do people give more honor to the government, their boss, or even themselves than they give to God?

4. Read Malachi 1:10. No man was willing to stand up and put a stop to the insufficient sacrifices being offered to God. How seriously do you take the holy worship of God?

5. God took no pleasure in their sacrifices and would not accept their offerings (1:10). Could you imagine ever hearing these words from God? Do you ever ask God if your worship and "sacrifices" are pleasing to Him?

6. God said His name is to be great among the nations. Read Acts 1:8. How has God planned for Christ's glorious name to be spread among the nations?

𝓤SE YOUR IMAGINATION

The children of Israel had seen bitter times, and that bitterness had turned into a doubt of God's love for them. Imagine a scenario of life that might give you pause over God's relationship with you. Have you ever felt so low over life circumstances that you doubted God's love for you? If you haven't, it may be hard to imagine ever feeling that way or sympathize with a person who is trying desperately to see God's love and mercy when her world is crashing around her. Whether it's imagining going through a difficult trial yourself, or helping a friend who is struggling through a dark valley, how would these verses remind you of the truth of God's love?

Romans 5:8

Ephesians 2:4–9

1 John 3:1

1 John 4:9

MORE PUSH AND PULL (MALACHI 2:1 TO 3:15)

What's really important to you? Don't answer too quickly; think about your allocation of time, money, and other resources. Consider your passions and interests. Now again: what is *really, really* important to you? For the priests hearing from God through Malachi, their answer should have been "to glorify the name of God," but instead, God's glory was not their priority. They did not and were not "taking *it* to heart" (Malachi 2:2 NASB).

Some of the priests of the past had served God in sincerity and truth, but the priests in Malachi's day fell short of the high honor of their calling. God promised to bring shame to them (2:3). Priests had the awesome responsibility to be the messengers of God; the people needed to be able to get wisdom based on God's law, instructing them how to live, but the priests weren't keepers of the law. The people were suffering because their very own priests were a stumbling block to them (2:8).

Next God proclaimed the children of Israel guilty before Him because of their sins concerning marriage. They had disobeyed God by intermarrying with pagan people who worshipped false gods (2:11), and they were practicing divorce (2:13–16).

Malachi 2:17 and 3:13–15 cover a similar topic, as God described the people's warped perceptions of God's justice. They complained that the wicked were prospering while they struggled, and their harsh words wearied God. Oh, how they failed to see their own sins! But in between these two bookends are gifts of hope from God. Despite their quarrelsome responses to God's reasoning, God offered life-giving words to the children of Israel:

God promised a forerunner (3:1). Malachi was the last prophet to speak before this promise was fulfilled in John the Baptist.

God promised the coming of Messiah (3:1). Through Jesus Christ would come restoration, righteousness, purification, and justice (3:2–5).

God made a conditional promise to those who would return to Him (3:7). God's promise reminds us that sin is a barrier between mankind and

God. "But your iniquities have separated you from your God; your sins have hidden his face from you, so that he will not hear" (Isaiah 59:2).

God made a conditional promise to pour out a blessing (3:8–12). While this promise came packaged with the accusation against the people for robbing God, what God offered them was good news. If the people would stop robbing God of tithes and offerings, God promised to pour out a blessing that was no less than a gift from heaven. Nature would yield bountiful crops, and the abundance of God's blessings would cause the nations to take notice of how much God loves His own special people.

*M*AJORING ON THE MINOR PROPHET

1. Read 1 Peter 2:9. If you are a Christian, you are a member of the royal priesthood. With this privileged post as a member of the priesthood, what has God called you to do in 1 Peter 2:9? Are you currently taking the calling to heart?

2. Read Malachi 2:7, which describes a priest's role concerning God's law and His great truths. How do you fulfill this great calling in your life?

3. Read 2 Corinthians 6:14. How does the marriage of a believer to an unbeliever create difficulty in producing "godly offspring" (Malachi 2:15)?

4. Think about the image of two people becoming one through marriage (Genesis 2:24; Malachi 2:15). With this image, how is divorce an act of violence (Malachi 2:16)?

5. Read Matthew 11:1–6. While John the Baptist was in prison, he sent his own disciples to talk with Jesus; John wanted to be certain that he had fulfilled his calling as the forerunner of Messiah. How would you convey to someone that Jesus is without a doubt the promised Savior of the world?

6. How is your faith strengthened by the many prophecies of the coming Messiah found in the Old Testament?

180

7. The children of Israel had suffered hard times, yet God still expected them to bring their tithes and offerings to Him. Are you ever tempted to give less than a tithe when you are struggling financially? How do God's words encourage you?

> Only 7 percent of American adults donate at least 10 percent of their income to a church or charitable institution. Age seems to be a factor in who gives; those over the age of 45 are almost twice as likely to give as those younger than 45.

U SE YOUR IMAGINATION

Most of us have learned to cope with criticism by tuning out the negative remarks of people we don't respect, but we are wise to listen carefully and evaluate the constructive criticism of people we respect. The most important feedback any of us will ever receive is what we hear from God. The priests were not listening to God's evaluations of their attitudes and actions, nor were the people of God yearning to honor God.

Take time to open your heart to the voice of God. Imagine yourself sitting at the feet of the Lord, asking the question, "Lord, are you pleased with me? Is my life an expression of worship before You? Am I bringing glory to Your great name?" Now listen. Be still and patient. What is Holy God saying to you?

REDEMPTION AND RECKONING (MALACHI 3:16 TO 4:6)

Yes, the Redeemer would arrive soon. In the midst of a discourse that sounded very similar to the many other times God had tried to reason with the rebellious children of Israel, the Lord of Hosts showed amazing grace to the rebellious Hebrews as well as the nations of the world. Not one Hebrew nor a single Gentile was worthy of the promise apart from God's gift of grace, yet all would be given the great gift of a Savior, this coming Messiah, who is Christ the Lord. Isn't God full of generosity to lavish such love upon all the earth? Isn't our God the epitome of patience, holding back His wrath and judgment and sending a Savior? Isn't God faithful to keep His promises, even though mankind is continually unfaithful to Him? God is good.

But not everyone will receive the promised Savior; God made this clear. And on God's day of redemption and reckoning that is yet to come, a distinction will be made between the righteous and the wicked, the servant of God and the one who will not bow the knee to his Maker. Jesus Himself talked of this distinction, saying that when He comes again in His glory He will divide the people of the nations as a shepherd divides sheep from goats (Matthew 25:31–33). For those who choose to live in opposition to God, destruction will come with devouring flames. But for the one who honors the name of God, heavenly sunshine, joyful frolicking, and victory is promised as a gift from the Lord.

God closed this message with intriguing information. God called for remembrance of His law given by Moses. Obedience always matters to God. Then God also promised that the prophet Elijah would appear "'before that great and dreadful day of the LORD comes'" (Malachi 4:5). God's promise is somewhat mysterious, and we have only to wait to see how this prophecy will be fulfilled. The Jews of Jesus' time were equally intrigued and mystified about this prophecy. John the Baptist was questioned by the religious authority of his day, but he clearly denied that he was this promised Elijah (John 1:19–21). Jesus also spoke of Elijah's coming (Matthew 17:11). Some scholars believe that Elijah could be one of the two witnesses described in Revelation 11:3–12.

*M*AJORING ON THE MINOR PROPHET

1. Read Malachi 3:16. Not all the Hebrews who heard God's message through Malachi were hardhearted. A group of them, perhaps what

might be considered a remnant, got together and spoke to one another about the goodness of the Lord. How did God respond? What does this verse reveal about what God finds noteworthy?

2. Referring to this remnant of people, what does God say He will call them (v. 17)? If you are a Christian, how does this knowledge affect the way you perceive your self-worth?

3. When you think about God dividing the goats from the sheep or the wicked from the righteous, are you certain of where you'll stand before God? (If you are unsure of where you stand, please turn to page 187 to read further about God's plan of salvation for you.) Do you know if your family and friends have a relationship with God?

$\mathcal{U}$ SE YOUR IMAGINATION

God's images of glory make our hearts leap for joy — how great are His promises for His children! Malachi 4:2–3 offers several hints of what is to come, including such ideas as healing, freedom, joyful frolic, satisfaction, and victory. Try to envision what the fulfillment of these words will be like.

Describe below what you imagine, and then try to fathom that "'eye has not seen, nor ear heard, nor have entered into the heart of man the things which God has prepared for those who love Him'" (1 Corinthians 2:9 NKJV).

$\mathcal{F}$INAL REFLECTIONS

Four hundred years of scriptural silence, and then a messenger named John arrived as a babe. Only months later, the Savior was born. The silence was broken. Oh, to be one of the shepherds receiving a message from the heavenly host on that long-awaited night — how the angels sang to proclaim the glory of God and the peace that had come down to man! All the Minor Prophets had spoken was wrapped up in the safe arrival of the newborn King. Then the perfect sacrifice of Christ on the Cross . . . then His conquering of death and the grave . . . but the best is yet to come. The completion of the message of the Minor Prophets is nearly upon us as we wait upon Christ's return. Lord Jesus, come!

> *Prayer: Precious Lord, do I look at Scripture and allow Your Words to penetrate my heart? God, reveal to me when I try to argue with Your Word. May I be quick to yield to Your Spirit and repent. May I keep praise on my lips all day long, and may I wait with joy and expectancy for my Savior to return! Amen.*

JOURNAL FOR THE MAJORS IN MY LIFE:

How to Become a Christian

God desires to have a personal relationship with you.

For I know the thoughts that I think toward you, says the Lord, thoughts of peace and not of evil, to give you a future and a hope (Jeremiah 29:11 NKJV).

But our sin separates us from God. All of us are sinners; no one can live up to God's holy standard, which is perfection.

For all have sinned and come short of the glory of God (Romans 3:23).

The penalty we deserve for our sin is spiritual death— total separation from God in hell.

For the wages of sin is death, but the gift of God is eternal life in Christ Jesus our Lord (Romans 6:23).

God is offering you the gift of eternal life through Jesus Christ.

"For God so loved the world that He gave His only begotten Son that whosoever believes in Him should not perish but have everlasting life" (John 3:16 NKJV).

Jesus Christ is the Son of God. He is the one and only bridge to God. Jesus said, *"I am the way, the truth, and the life. No one comes to the Father except through me"* (John 14:6).

Jesus lived a sinless life. He allowed Himself to be nailed to the Cross to pay the price for our sins so we would not have to face hell. What a wonderful act of love! He died on the Cross, was buried, and then rose from the grave. *But God demonstrates His own love toward us, in that while we were still sinners, Christ died for us* (Romans 5:8 NKJV).

God is offering you new life in Jesus Christ. Do you want to become a Christian? Then through prayer to God:

1. Admit you are a sinner, asking for forgiveness and turning from your sins.

2. Confess that Jesus, the Son of God, died on the Cross and rose again to save you from your sins.

3. Invite Jesus to be the Lord and Savior of your life.

   Dear God, I know that I am a sinner. I am asking for Your forgiveness, and I want to turn away from my sins. I believe that Jesus, Your Son, died on the Cross and rose again to save me from my sins, and I now put my trust in Him as my personal Lord and Savior. Amen.

"Whoever calls upon the name of the Lord shall be saved" (Romans 10:13 NKJV).

If you have prayed to receive Christ, you have been given forgiveness and eternal life!

Major Truths Notes